Name It and Claim It!

by

Dr. Frederick K.C. Price

Harrison House
Tulsa, Oklahoma

Unless otherwise indicated, all scripture quotations are taken from the *King James Version* of the Bible.

4th Printing
Over 43,000 in Print

Contents

Introduction

Proverbs 18:21

Death and life are in the power of the tongue: and they that love it shall eat the fruit thereof.

Proverbs 18:21 tells me that with my tongue I can speak *death* to my life and I can speak life to my life. My life then, is controlled by my tongue. *Death and life, life and death are in the power of the tongue.*

This principle of death and life being in the power of the tongue, I call "the power of positive confession."

Let me define the word *confession* as I will be using it in this book, so that we will be in one accord. But first, I want to ask you a question and I want you to be honest about the answer: What is the first thing that comes to your mind as you read the words, "the power of positive confession"? You probably thought about a *negative*, right?

If you ask the average person, in 99.9% of the cases, you will find that the word *confession* is always associated with a negative, usually sin. It is usually thought of in the context of "Father, forgive me. I blew it. I messed up. I did something wrong." That is our normal "thinking" about the word *confession*. In other words, there is more said in the average church about a negative confession than there is about a positive confession. In fact, from childhood, we are conditioned to the negative, more than we are to the positive. This idea of negative rather than positive associated with the word *confession* is instilled in our children.

We, as the children of God, however, need to recognize that there is more in the Bible about a positive confession than there is about a negative confession.

5

Now, to our definition: The Greek word for *confession* is *homologeo,* and it means "to agree with" or "say the same thing that God says about you and/or your circumstances." It does not mean, per se, to confess a negative. Most of the time, however, we are confessing something bad, something negative, something that we have done wrong.

Do not misunderstand me, though. If you have done something wrong, you ought to confess it. But we should not spend our whole life confessing wrong. We ought to be living in such a way that there is very little that we should *have* to confess.

In this book, my desire is to share with you what I believe God means by confession, what the Word says about confession, and how what you say or confess with your tongue can affect every aspect of your life. I trust you will learn that through your confession, you will add life to your life, or death to your life. My desire is that you begin to speak *life* to your life.

1

Positive Confession — Positive Thinking

Proverbs 18:21 is the biblical foundation for the principle of death and life being in the power of the tongue. I call this life and death principle "the power of positive confession." What principle could be more powerful and more vital to the people of God?

The primary thing that we do with our tongue is speak, or talk. We would have a very difficult time talking or verbalizing without a tongue. Yes, it is true that we use our tongue to eat and that our taste buds are located on our tongue, but generally, we talk more than we eat. Or we *should*! You have a real problem if you eat more than you talk. And maybe that is the problem with some people! Christianity is actually a confession, from the beginning to the end, whether we like it or not. And true Christianity is a positive confession. I did not say *true* Christianity was positive thinking, although positive *thinking* can play a role in our positive confessions.

Some years ago, there was a book written by Norman Vincent Peale, which was a best-seller all over the world. It was titled *The Power of Positive Thinking.* I submit to you that it is certainly good to think positively. There is no question that you will be better off in life if you learn to think positively. But I believe that positive thinking is only the first stage of something bigger. If positive thinking is all that you are ever exposed to, that is well and good. Because that is better than being exposed only to negative thinking.

However, if all you ever do is *think* positively, you will never learn how to *speak* positively.

You must start out from a premise of positive thinking. But if all you do is think positively and never move into the *next* stage, then you will stay — as far as your circumstances are concerned — in the same environment. All that will happen is that you will have a better attitude. You will be able to smile while the ship is sinking, instead of wringing your hands, crying, screaming and hollering!

But if you learn how to *speak* positively based on the Word of God, you can keep the ship afloat! And that is the major difference.

Thinking positively instead of negatively is better, there is no question about that. But, we want to go on to God's best. Positive thinking is absolutely correct. It is right. It is proper. It is good, and that is where we start, but that is *not* where we *end*. If you only *think* positively, all you will do is affect your attitude about your circumstances, but you will not *change* them. When they amputate your leg, because of positive thinking, you will be able to deal with it without climbing the wall. You will be able to accept it by rationalizing, "God must have a purpose in this." Or, "I can get an artificial leg and still function." You might rationalize, "Thank God I'm not dead. Thank God I didn't go to the cemetery. I'll be limited in what I can do, but thank God, I'm not dead." You will affect yourself in that way, but I believe that if you learn the secret of positive confession, you can change your circumstances, and that is what is important.

What Is "Confession"?

Confession in Greek means that you "agree with" or "say the same thing that God says about you and/or your circumstances." Do you realize that the only way you can get saved is by confession? "Oh, no, Brother Price, you don't get saved by confession, you get saved by believing." That is partially true; believing is involved, but if you do not confess what you believe, you still will not get saved. That statement may not be denominational or theological, but it is biblical.

Salvation involves confession and has nothing to do with emotions. Yet, in most cases, we as Christians have been guided toward emotion rather than confession.

In most churches, we are usually told that if we confess our sins the Lord will save us, and that is untrue. That is not the way you get saved. Nowhere in God's Word does He require the sinner to confess his sins, *so that he can get saved*. That is not taught in the Bible. It is taught in personal ministry classes in some churches. It is taught in certain kinds of evangelistic outreaches. It is taught in certain Sunday School quarterlies, but it is not taught in the Bible.

You ought to thank God that He does not require you to confess your sins in order to get saved, because if He did, then you would have to confess *every one* of them in order to get saved. You could not leave one out because the concept is not to confess *some* of your sins, but to confess your sin(s). That is plural. That means every one of them! It is just like dialing a telephone number. There are seven numbers, and if you leave one of the numbers out, you do not get the party you are calling. It is like a combination lock: If you leave one of the numbers out, you do not open the lock.

Let me say this to you, so that you will get it straight for the rest of your life. When you glibly say, "Lord, forgive me of my sins," that amounts to nothing at all. "Forgive me of my sins." What sins? Which ones do you need to be forgiven of? I do not need to be forgiven of the sin of adultery, because I have never committed that sin. So, why include that in my prayer? I must specify what I want to be forgiven of.

I should be confessing what I have sinned, so that I can be forgiven of the sin. So, to say, "Lord, forgive me of my sins," is not biblical. I know it is traditional — people do it all the time, but that is *not* why you got saved.

Nowhere in the Bible does God require the sinner to confess his sins *in order to get saved.* I know there is a verse in 1 John 1:9 which says, **If we confess our sins, he is faithful and just to forgive us our sins, and to cleanse us from all unrighteousness.** That verse has been taken out of its setting and applied to sinners, although it is not even for sinners. John was not writing to sinners, he was writing to Christians. He said, **My little children....** We have taken that verse out of its setting and used it as a ministering tool for sinners, saying, "If you confess your sins, God will forgive you." No! You *may* go through all of that, but that is not why God forgave you.

The fact is, God really does not actually forgive the sinner's sins in order to be in a position to save the sinner. In a very broad sense, yes, God forgives the sinner's sins, but that is not really what salvation is based on.

What God actually does with the sinner's sins is to **remit** them. The Apostle Peter began that message on the day of Pentecost (Acts 2:38). He said,

> ...**Repent, and be baptized every one of you in the name of Jesus Christ for the** *remission* (not for the forgiveness) **of sins, and ye shall receive the gift of the Holy Ghost.**

Remission means to send it away from you. You receive a bill from the department store or wherever, and it says, "Please enclose this stub with your *remittance.*" Your remittance is something you are going to send away from you. What God does is send the sinner's sin away from him. He really does not forgive it. He remits it. He treats it as though it never was! Technically, the only sins that God *forgives* are Christians' sins.

There is a confession that the sinner must make in order to get saved, but it is not a confession of sin.

Let me say it again: Christianity is a confession, but not a confession of sin. God does not require sinners to confess their sins in order to get saved. First John 1:9 is not for sinners. Technically, it is for Christians. Let us look at that scripture more closely.

1 John 1:9

If we confess our sins, he is faithful and just to forgive us our sins, and to cleanse us from all unrighteousness.

Unrighteousness is the word righteousness with the prefix "un," which means "non-righteous." The scripture says, **If we confess our sins** (s-i-n-s), **He is faithful and just to forgive us our sins, and to cleanse us from all unrighteousness.**

Question: What do you normally clean up? You usually clean something that is dirty. But wait a minute! What can get dirty? Something that is *already* clean. If there was never any clean, there could not be any dirty. So, cleanse implies dirty.

Cleanse us from all unrighteousness would imply that the individual who is confessing his sins was once righteous. He sinned and the sin dirtied his righteousness and the end result was unrighteousness. If you confess your sins, God will clean you up and wash away the dirty, and when you wash away the dirty, you do away with the "un" and you have righteousness left. Obviously the unrighteousness was first of all righteousness.

That could not be talking about sinners, because they have never been righteous. You cannot be righteous unless you are born again, unless you are a child of God, having accepted Jesus as your personal Savior and Lord.

Second Corinthians 5:21 informs us that *He who knew no sin was made to be sin for us that we might be made the*

11

righteousness of God in Him. By accepting Jesus as your personal Savior and Lord, you become a righteous person. Sinners never had any righteousness, so they could never be cleaned up from it.

Christians **have** or **are** righteousness, but we can sin. When we sin, it is really not that we lose our righteousness, but we lose our sense or consciousness of righteousness, and we do not ''feel'' righteous anymore.

You lose your *sense* of righteousness, but you do not lose your righteousness (which means right-standing with God), any more than your child loses you as the mother or the father, just because he went into that cookie jar and took those chocolate chip cookies when you told him not to. He took the cookies and you may have to correct him, but he is still your child. I do not care what that boy does, that is still your child! He can go to court and have his name legally changed, but it does not change the fact that he is still your child.

What Must the Sinner Do About His Sin?

If you birthed that child, there is nothing *anybody* in this world can do to change it. Changing your name does not change your birth. So, if you are a child of God when you sin, you do not lose your sonship or relationship, but you break your fellowship. Sin breaks fellowship.

I want to say it again: 1 John 1:9 is for Christians, not for sinners. If 1 John 1:9 is not for sinners, what is the sinner supposed to do about his sins? REPENT! FORSAKE THEM! STOP! in the name of the Law of God. The sinner is supposed to confess Romans 10:9,10:

> **That if thou shalt confess with thy mouth the Lord Jesus** (it does not say confess your sins), **and shalt believe in thine heart that God hath raised him from the dead, thou shalt be saved.** (Sin is not mentioned here.)

For with the heart man believeth unto righteousness; and with the mouth *confession* is made unto salvation.

Notice that salvation comes by your mouth, not by confessing *sins,* but by confessing Jesus. Christianity is confession — from beginning to end. You confess your way into the Kingdom of God with your mouth, and then you confess your way to the top of righteousness and victorious living in Christ.

Never Give Up Saying and Believing

Matthew 10:32,33 Jesus is speaking — think of it in reference to confession:

Whosoever therefore shall (what?) **confess me before men** (that means in front of men because God does not have any secret disciples), **him will I confess also before my Father which is in heaven.** (In other words, if you talk about Me unashamedly in front of men, I will talk about you unashamedly in front of My heavenly Father.)

But whosoever shall deny me before men, him will I also deny before my Father which is in heaven.

We read in Proverbs that death and life are in the power of the tongue. Now look at John 12:42,43:

Nevertheless among the chief rulers also many believed on him; but because of the Pharisees they did not *confess* him, lest they should be put out of the synagogue:

For they loved the praise of men more than the praise of God.

There is a price to pay to make a positive confession in line with the Word of God. Hebrews 10:23 says **Let us hold fast the profession of our faith without wavering; (for he is faithful that promised).** The word profession in this verse is actually the same Greek word for confession. It should read, Let us hold fast the *confession* of our faith without wavering; (for he is faithful that promised). In other words, do not give up saying and believing. I will add *believing* because that goes with it.

Never give up saying what you hope. Do you have a hope that is consistent with God's plan and purpose? If so, keep saying it. Hebrews 10:35,36 says:

> **Cast not away therefore your confidence, which hath great recompense of reward.**

> **For ye have need of patience, that, after ye have done the will of God, ye might receive the promise.**

The word *might* in verse 36 should actually be *may*. Now what is your confidence? Your confidence is your hope spoken of in the 23rd verse of Hebrews 10. And what is your hope? Your hope is in what God said in His Word, and the Bible says that God's Word is forever settled in heaven. The Bible says that not one jot or tittle will fall from God's Word until all be fulfilled.

You can count on whatever you base your hope on, that is in line with God's Word, so hold fast to that. Now what is the will of God? The will of God is whatever God tells you to do in reference to whatever it is you are believing God for.

You have to find scripture and then whatever that scripture tells you, hold on to that. For example, let us say that a husband and wife want to get into agreement and believe God for a certain thing. They want to pool their faith, or put it together, in other words. They would use a scripture like Matthew 18:19 ...**That if two of you shall agree on earth as touching any thing that they shall ask, it shall be done for them of my Father which is in heaven.** That would be the will of God for more than one person who wants to get in agreement with another person. Do not cast that away.

14

2
You Shall Have What You Say

We will look at another verse of scripture that deals with confession, and then I will show you how to determine the will of God.

Mark 11:23, Jesus is speaking:

> For verily I say unto you, That whosoever shall (what?) **say unto this mountain, Be thou removed, and be thou cast into the sea; and shall not doubt in his heart, but shall believe that those things which he saith shall come to pass; he shall have whatsoever he saith.**

Confession is saying, and saying is confession. Now your heart is your spirit, that is your inner man. That is the *real* you. Notice that in Mark 11:23 when the word "believe" is used the second time, the word "heart" is not mentioned with it. But it is obvious that if He does not want you to doubt in the heart, He must want you to do the believing in the same place where He does not want the doubt.

As a result, I think it is a safe assumption — and that we do no injustice to the scripture to paraphrase it and say it this way, . . . *and shall not doubt in his heart, but shall believe in his heart. . . .* Can you see that? Doubt is the opposite of believing. If you are believing, you are not doubting; if you are doubting, you are not believing.

Notice again, He says, . . . **but shall believe in his heart that those things which he saith** (*or confesseth*) **shall come to pass.** They have not come to pass yet, because if they had already come to pass, you would not have to say it, because you would have it. Shall come is future tense —

future to the saying of it, future to the believing of it in your heart. If you already had it, you would not have to believe it. This is the rule, this is the will of God.

What Is The Will Of God?

The will of God is that you have to say it with your mouth and you have to believe it in your heart without any doubt. As a result, Jesus said, ...**You shall have**.... He did not say you shall have whatever you *need*, He said you shall have whatever you *say*. We must be careful here, because Jesus is enunciating a Divine, Universal Law. We must remember that laws can work for you, but the same law can also work against you if you do not observe the conditions that cause the law to operate.

If I plug my television set into the electrical outlet, I can watch the "Ever Increasing Faith" TV program and be ministered to. But if I take my fingers and wet them and stick them into the wall socket, that same electricity that will allow me to watch "Ever Increasing Faith" will also allow me to ever increasingly die! I would not be observing the law.

If you form the habit of saying negative things, even jokingly, then where do you separate the joke from the reality? When does it get to the point where you are really "saying" *out of your heart*? Because you have formed the habit of saying negative things so much, after a while, you begin to apply that negativism to the positive things that you want to say and you will end up getting the wrong thing.

Think about this; I am almost sure you have done this, because most of us have: You go to the restaurant, the waiter or waitress comes over, hands you the menu and asks if anybody wants anything to drink. Cocktail or whatever. They do not know who you are, so they assume that you want something to drink. You might say, yes, coffee, coke, or something like that. Then he or she might say, "I'll give you a little time to look at the menu." You then select what you want from the menu. The waiter or waitress then returns and says, "Are you ready to order?" "Yes, I believe I will have chicken fricassee." Or, "Yes, I believe I will have shrimp scampi."

"I BELIEVE I will have...I BELIEVE...." "Come on! No, you do not believe it, you are going to have it. *That* is what you want. "I *will* have, "Or, "I think I'll try...." " You are not going to try it, you are going to order it. You are going to eat it. Is that not right? I WANT shrimp scampi, and I intend to eat shrimp scampi until the eating tells me I do not like it. Then the eating will stop on scampi and I will order something else, or I will not come back to that restaurant anymore.

Consider Mark 11:23: If all you do is *believe* you will have scampi, you will never get it. You will have to say it. You will have to confess it to the waiter or the waitress or you will not get it! They will not allow you into the kitchen to cook your own food at the restaurant!

Therefore I say unto you that whosoever shall *say* . . . With this verse, Jesus is enunciating a law, and as amazing as it may sound, this law will work for sinners as well as it will for Christians. The difference is that for the non-Christian, there is no life in it, but it will still work. Two plus two is four if you are a sinner or a Christian, because that is a mathematical law. It is a principle. If the worst person in the world adds up a column of figures, 2 + 2 will still come out to 4, because that is a principle.

Develop A Habit Of Speaking Positively

Christians need to learn how to be positive. But positive in line with God's plan and purpose. I am not talking about the power of positive thinking just as some kind of esoteric regimen. That is good, but it is not good enough for us to achieve what God would have us to achieve.

That is the point I want to make. Thinking positively is always better than thinking negatively, and it will put you in a better frame of mind to accept what is going on around you, but it is not going to change anything. But the power of positive confession, in line with God's Word, will change the circumstances.

Jesus said, in Mark 11:23:

> **For verily I say unto you, That whosoever shall say unto this mountain, Be thou removed, and be thou cast into the sea; and shall not doubt in his heart, but shall believe that those things which he saith shall come to pass; he shall have whatsoever he saith.**

That means you will have the negative as well as the positive. If you do not want the negative, you had better stop saying the negative.

Why not say something that will help reinforce in me positive ideas so that I develop it into a habit. When I get to a situation in life, I do not have to say, "What shall I say now?" I don't want to say "Take care." I don't want to say "She makes me sick." When I develop a habit of speaking positively, I will not have to say that, because it will become as easy as breathing, an automatic reflex action. According to Mark 11:23, the will of God is to say it with your mouth and believe it in your heart.

I want to show you a mathematical equation so that you will understand how important the things I have stated are. If the number of times a thing is repeated is any indication of its importance, then we need to be very careful that we learn the lessons that the Spirit of God is showing us in the Word of God. As we read Mark 11:23 again, I will point out this mathematical equation:

> **For verily I say unto you, That whosoever shall (1) say unto this mountain, Be thou removed, and be**

thou cast into the sea; and shall not doubt in his heart, but shall (1) believe that those things which he (2) saith shall come to pass; he shall have whatsoever he (3) saith.

Notice the ratio, 3 to 1. Jesus only mentions "believing" one time, but he mentions "saying" something three times. I wonder, is the Man trying to tell us something? YES! He knew that Christians would not have a problem with the believing part because they will believe anything, even a lie.

People do not have a problem with believing. But where they fall short is "saying." "Honey, you ain't gonna get me to say that! I ain't gonna say that I got something I can't see. You ain't gonna make no fool out of me!"

Jesus knew that people would not have a problem believing. Their problem would be confessing or saying. Inhibitions, self-centeredness, not wanting to look different to other people are problems for most people. Now we will dress like a fool and look different, but for some reason, that does not bother us. But when it comes to saying something that is different, that is a problem. When it comes to the things of God, most people suddenly have this great spirit of sincerity rising up in them. This great "honesty" spirit comes on them, and this great desire to be perfectly circumspect. Yet, oftentimes they say they have things that they do not have and never think anything about it.

Here's an example:

"Say man, I haven't seen you in a long time. When are you going to give me my five dollars you told me you were going to pay me three weeks ago?"

"See me Friday, I'll have some money Friday."

You are telling a lie. Friday has not come yet. The company you work for may go bankrupt and you will not have any money on Friday. But you are already confessing the future, and you have no problem with that.

19

"Meet me right here outside the gate, and I will have my paycheck on Friday."

We do not have a problem with that because we believe the word of men. The man *told* you he was going to pay you on Friday. The man always says and does what he says he is going to do; but God, you cannot count on God. If God says it shall come to pass, it may not. We have great confidence in the words of men and based on their word, we will go out telling it all over town.

The power of positive confession works. If you believe that it shall come to pass, you have to *say* it. We receive what we say if we believe it in our heart. THAT IS THE WORD OF GOD! That law, Mark 11:23, will work for you if you are a saint or a sinner, because it is a law. As long as you are functioning inside the law, that law is going to work for you.

For verily I say unto you, that *whosoever*... It did not say "whosoever Christian, whosoever preacher, whosoever minister," but rather, whosoever shall *say*. Are you a whosoever? If you did not know it, I am! I am a WHOSOEVER, so he was talking to me. He said, WHOSOEVER shall *say*, not *hope*. "Well, I'm hoping." No, whosoever shall *say!* "Well, I think...." He did not say *think*. He said, whosoever shall *say*.

YES! EVEN TO THE MOUNTAIN, BE THOU REMOVED, AND BE THOU CAST INTO THE SEA; AND SHALL NOT DOUBT IN HIS HEART, BUT SHALL BELIEVE THAT THOSE THINGS WHICH HE *SAITH* SHALL COME TO PASS; HE SHALL HAVE WHATSOEVER HE SAITH.

Positive or negative, you will have it, if you believe it and *say* it. I repeat again, we need to develop the habit of speaking life instead of death to our lives. Proverbs 6:2 states:

Thou art snared with the words of thy mouth, thou art taken with the words of thy mouth.

You Are Snared With the Words of Your Mouth

Think about it — you are snared or trapped with the words of your mouth. Remember, we have an adversary, Satan, and he is a legalist and will snare you or trap you with *your* words. Proverbs 6:2 did not say you are snared by the thoughts of your head. It does not become a trap until you say it with your mouth. You could think some thoughts that could ultimately be a trap, if you acted on it. But it is your mouth that springs that trap!

1 Peter 5:8:

> **Be sober, be vigilant; because your adversary the devil, as a roaring lion, walketh about, seeking whom he may devour.**

How will he devour you? With the words of your mouth. Satan will keep you bound, poor, sick, and oppressed by the words of your mouth. When you make such negative confessions as "I think I'm gonna be sick. I hear the Hong Kong Flu is on the way, it'll probably stop at my house." Or, "They have invited us over for dinner and they'll probably have seafood and seafood always makes me sick."

We say things like that, thinking that we are being honest and telling the truth. You don't realize that is how the devil got control of you in the first place in terms of cheating you out of seafood, or whatever. Because you got sick *one* time, the devil put a thought in your mind that it was the shrimp you ate that made you sick; or the lobster or sea bass is what made you sick. He programmed you through your mind and got you to say it with your mouth.

You should not have any problems eating whatever you want to eat. There may be some things you choose not to eat, but not because it makes you sick.

21

A true confession of faith
always agrees with the Word of God.

Remember that what you confess or say with your mouth is your faith speaking, and it will reveal whether your faith is weak or strong. You can measure a person by their words. Jesus said one time, and it is true, **. . . for out of the abundance of the heart the mouth speaketh** (Matt. 12:34). Whatever is there in abundance will come out through your mouth.

When your confession agrees with the Word of God, then and only then will you receive what God has promised you. A true confession of faith is always based on the Word of the Living God. That is why Satan has so cleverly kept the Word of God out of the churches, because Satan knows that if people ever find out about the Word of God and begin to believe in their heart that what they say with their mouth will come to pass, then he will be finished lording it over them. He will no longer have control over their lives. He will no longer be able to snare them with their words.

God has designed His system to work by His Word. That is why He gave it to us. Not to adorn your coffee table. Not to be placed on the mantelpiece. Not to hold the little rose that George gave you on your first date. That is *not* what the Bible is for. God gave us His Word so that we would know His Word, so that we would *believe* His Word, so that we would say His Word, so that He could confirm His Word in our lives. That is the way the system works.

Mark 16:19,20:

So then after the Lord had spoken unto them (that is the disciples), **he was received up into heaven, and sat on the right hand of God.**

And they went forth, and preached every where, the Lord working with them, and *confirming the word* **with signs following.**

Now notice what it does not say. It does *not* say that he *confirmed them.* It said they preached the Word, but God did not confirm them that preached the Word. God confirmed His Word preached. It says signs *following.* Word *first,* then the *signs.*

What most people want is to see some signs first and then they will believe. They say something like, ''Well, if I ever see somebody get healed, then I will believe that divine healing is real.'' But it doesn't work that way. You have to believe it first, then you see it. When you see something, why in the world would you have to *believe* it?! It is obvious that you would know it then. ''Well, after all, seein' is believin'.'' No, it is not! Seeing is knowing. Seeing is not believing, seeing is *knowing.*

''I'll believe it when I see it.'' Many have said that all their lives. They have heard that from childhood. But it has nothing to do with seeing anything. You have to believe it for no other reason than the fact that the Almighty God said it. You have to believe it and then you have to say it, if you want God to get involved in it. That is what makes it work. So, our confession must agree with the Word of God.

A TRUE CONFESSION OF FAITH ALWAYS AGREES WITH THE WORD OF GOD. Remember this and never forget it; *when my confession agrees with the Word of God, THEN I will receive what God has promised me.*

Using sickness as an illustration, if you keep hearing all your life that God has put that sickness on you to make a better person out of you, that God put that illness on you to help to develop you, then you get the idea that God is behind sickness and disease and He is not. God wants you well, not sick!

But how can you agree with God when you do not know what He says? And so, you go around saying, ''Well, the Lord put this on me. I know God is testing me.'' And

God is not involved in it. He cannot confirm that, because it is not His Word. So, as a result, you are trapped by the words of your mouth, snared by your words. You are speaking death to your life instead of life — and you do not even know it!

3

God Cannot Lie!

Since the original Greek word for the word *confession* as it is used in the New Testament means "to agree with," or "say the same thing that God says," I will be continually referring to this fact throughout this book.

The Bible says that it is impossible for God to lie. If it is impossible for God to lie, the only alternative is that God *must* tell the truth. So, if God says something about me, then that must be who I am, what I have, and what I can do. If God says I can do it, I can do it. If God says I have it, I have it. If God says that is who I am, then that is who I am.

At the time that I find out what God says about me or the situation, I might not be experiencing any of it in my personal life, but that is irrelevant and immaterial. That is still who I am, because God sees the end from the beginning, and the beginning from the end. And since He cannot lie, but *only* tell the truth, then that must be who I am.

If I will have the spiritual sense to bring my mouth, my confession — the words that I say — into line with what God says I am, I have, and I can do — the things that I find in His Word — I will have that manifested in my personal everyday life. That is exactly the way it works. That is a divine law. We need to form the habit — and we need to stay with it — of agreeing with what God says.

I do not know about you, but I have been down and now I am up, and up is better! I have been sick and now

I am well, and well is better. Learning about confession has so dramatically changed my life — the difference between what I was before I found out about confession and what I have become since I found out about it is so dramatic. It is almost as dramatic as the change between when I was a sinner and when I accepted Christ and received salvation. So I have personally experienced what I am talking about in regard to confession. I am not giving you theory, or ''I think,'' ''It could be,'' ''Maybe so if all other conditions are met.'' I am telling you what I know to be true!

Even though I began to operate in this law of confession, it sounded strange to me when I first heard it. How could what I *say* have anything to do with what I have and what I experience in my life? But God said it, so I began to say it. I said, ''I don't have anything to lose, I'm already down for the count. The enemy's standing in my chest with his boot on my neck.'' I had absolutely nothing to lose.

So twenty years ago (prior to the writing of this book), I began saying what God said, and I am telling you the truth, it was miraculous, the change that took place in my own personal life. As a result, I am committed to the proposition that this is one of the most important truths that God has revealed to us in His Word, and yet, it is so misunderstood.

Name It and Claim It — Or You Get Nothing!

Every once in awhile, there are some who make fun of, poke fun at, and criticize this law of confession. A minister was heard to say this about yours truly, Fred Price: ''That's the 'Name it and Claim it' bunch!'' Hey! If that is who I am, I accept, because it is true. It *is* name it and claim it.

I do not deal with the criticizers because of the criticism, but to show you how people can miss God. To illustrate: when you go to the Will Call, you had better name and claim what is yours, or you will not get anything. ''I bought a bicycle. It's red. It's an ABC bicycle made on Mars. Here's my receipt, I want it!'' I named and claimed it and that is what they gave me. They did not bring me an elephant, or a hippopotamus, or a rhinoceros, or a speed boat. They brought me a bicycle, a red bicycle because that is the one I bought and that is the receipt I have, showing that I paid for it. I named it, I claimed it, and I got it!

If I had walked up to the Will Call window and said, ''Hey, I want to pick up my merchandise,'' they would have said, ''What's your name?'' ''I have no name.'' ''Well, what's the merchandise?'' ''I don't know.''

If this scenario had taken place, what would I have received? An example like that, we have no problem understanding. We can see that because we are so intelligent, so erudite and scholarly. But when it comes to the things of God, suddenly it is a dilemma for us.

Name it and claim it?! You better believe it! I am the name it and claim it man! Everything I have truly desired over the last 20 years (prior to the writing of this book) that I have truly desired, I have named it, claimed it, and I got it. So, maybe it just works for me. Maybe I am God's special child!

Your Uncle Rufus, a multimillionaire, whom you have not seen in 25 years, died and left you 10 million dollars. You had better go name it and claim it or you will not get it!

You had better go wherever the will is being read and let those folk know, ''Hey, I'm the one Uncle Rufus was talking about! Here's my I.D. I claim my inheritance!''

You name and claim what God said you can name and claim. You do not just arbitrarily go off and name and claim something. When you park your car, they give you a claim check. When you come back, you cannot say, ''I want that Rolls Royce sitting over there.''

Do you think they are going to give you that car? No way! They will only give you the one you have a claim check for. You have a claim check that matches the one that is stuck under your windshield wiper blade. The numbers had better match up or he is a fool if he gives you that car!

...there is a negative end to laws
as well as a positive end.

Remember, all laws have a reciprocal. They all work in reverse. Did you know that? In other words, there is a negative end to laws as well as a positive end. Many people do not realize that, and everything they have in life is because of what they have named and claimed over the years.

You must realize that laws work whether you know they are working or not. Laws are not laws and valid because you know them. They work whether you know they are working or not.

In our society, we have been programmed — without realizing it — to name it and claim it. People told us something about ourselves and we named it and claimed it: "I'll never amount to anything, because none of the males in our family have ever amounted to anything. They have all been failures, so I'll probably be a failure." "Granddaddy was a wino, my daddy was an alcoholic and I'll probably be one, too."

You named that and claimed that. "We have never had anything in our family, we've always been poor. I'm a third generation welfare recipient. My kids will probably be fourth generation welfare recipients." Again, they named it and claimed it. They did not know that was what they were doing, but a rose by any other name is still a rose.

1 John 1:9:

If we confess our sins, he is faithful and just to forgive us our sins, and to cleanse us from all unrighteousness.

God is the One Who wrote that Word. He said, **If we confess our sins, he is faithful and just to forgive us.** That means that when I sin, I have to say I sinned, and it is not until I say I have sinned that I get the forgiveness.

God says certain things are sin. For instance, fornication is sin. God said it in His Word. If I commit fornication, when I say that it is a sin, then I am agreeing with God, and only then will I be forgiven. If God says that stealing is a sin, you have to say, "Stealing is a sin." If you steal, then you have to say, "I have sinned" and it is not until then that you will receive forgiveness.

Psalm 103:1-3:

Bless the Lord, O my soul: and all that is within me, bless his holy name.

Bless the Lord, O my soul, and forget not all his benefits:

Who forgiveth all thine iniquities; who healeth all thy diseases.

From that scripture, it is obvious there is a discrepancy between the traditionally-held idea that God is the One Who makes us sick for some divine purpose. If God is the One Who makes us sick as well as the One Who heals all our diseases, we have a problem. Healing cancels out disease and sickness, and whatever benefit God had in mind for making us sick is lost! Very smart of God, indeed.

Psalm 103:1-3 clearly shows that God is not in the business of making us sick. God is the healer, not the afflictor — even though He has been accused of it traditionally.

Notice what the third verse says: **Who forgiveth all thine iniquities; who healeth all thy diseases.** When a sickness or a disease attacks my body, even though the circumstances may say I am sick, I have to say what God says about that condition if I am going to be released from it. If I say, "I am sick," then I am saying that it is mine. What I have to do is say, "I believe what God says. I believe I am healed of this condition. I believe I am well."

That is what we must say if we are going to get that healing physically manifested in our lives. In James 5:14,15, it says, **Is any sick among you? let him call for the elders of the church; and let them pray over him, anointing him with oil in the name of the Lord: And the prayer of faith shall save the sick, and the Lord** (just might raise him up?) **shall raise him up** (That means will, isn't that right?); **and if he have committed sins, they shall be forgiven him.**

Understand this, you do not have to anoint people with oil. That is just one of the many methods God has placed in the Body of Christ, because He wants us healed. People are at varying levels of spiritual understanding, and while one method would work on one level, it would not work on another level.

God has made enough methods available so that wherever you are in terms of your knowledge and spiritual development, there is a method that can reach you. The highest method, of course, is to believe God for yourself. God says He will raise me up. I have to say that, and then practice that, that is, anoint with oil for this method to work.

1 Peter 2:24:

> **Who his own self bare our sins in his own body on the tree, that we, being dead to sins, should live unto righteousness: by whose stripes ye were healed.**

If you know anything about elementary English, you know that the word "were" is a past tense term, and is indicative of the fact that the time of action has already taken place. It is *not taking place*, it is *not going to take place*, it is already *an accomplished fact!* "Were healed."

As I said before, God cannot lie. The only alternative is that God tells the truth. If God says I am healed with Jesus' stripes, then either I am healed or God is a liar. If I was, I am. And if I *am*, I *is*. That is not good English, but the word "is" says you know that we are talking about n-o-w, *now!*

In all of the churches that I matriculated through over a 17-year period, I was never told that I was supposed to say what God said about me. I thought I was supposed to say what the circumstances said about me, what the doctor said about me, what the newspapers said about me, what the history books said about me, what the white folks said about me, what the black folks said about me. I thought I was supposed to say what my mama, my friends, and my enemies said about me.

I did not know I was supposed to say what my Heavenly Father said about me, so I *never* said what He said about me. When the circumstances came in like a flood and said I was sick, I said, "I'm SICK!" "How do you feel?" "I'm SICK!" "You don't look too well." "I'm SICK!" "Are you going to work today?" "I'm SICK!"

I confessed that, because I was a truthful person. I wanted to tell the truth. I did not want to deliberately lie. The circumstances told me I was sick, because I was hurting. But all the time that was going on, God's Word never changed. It said the same thing. BY *WHOSE STRIPES YE WERE HEALED.* That tells me that I am healed *NOW.* Did you notice what that does not say? It does not say "By whose stripes ye were healed *when ye feel like ye are healed.* " It does not say "By whose stripes ye were healed *if ye look like ye were healed.* " It says, **By whose stripes ye were healed.**

So, I started saying that. I figured I had nothing to lose. If confession does not work, I am going to be sick anyway, so I might as well say it. I began to say, "I BELIEVE I am healed.'' And, do you know, circumstances began to change! Do you know that in the 17 years (prior to the writing of this book) that I have been pastor of Crenshaw Christian Center, I have never missed a Sunday morning ministering the Word — other than when I was either on a cruise or on a tour to Israel with the church or on vacation. Other than that, I have never missed being at my job on a Sunday morning. I have never missed my Tuesday night or Friday morning Bible class because of any physical condition, because I believe I am well.

I never said I was not *attacked*. I never said that there are not times that I am experiencing pain. There have been many times when I have been ministering and felt like 17 miles of unpaved road. Every step I took and every word I spoke was painful. I have to agree in my heart, my spirit, with what God says and I have noticed that when I do that, that is when I experience the anointing of God's power to put me over. If I were to ever stop and wait until I feel perfectly well before I initiate any activity, I would never feel well. Satan would have me right where he wants me. I have to act like I am well.

What would I do if I were actually well, with not a pain in my body, nothing hindering me physically? I would be doing my job. I would be going on vacation, making love to my wife, hugging my kids, playing with the frog — if I had a frog, petting the dog — if I had a dog, and stroking the cat — if I had a cat. I would be doing what I normally do, right? God said with His stripes I was healed. I believe what God said, so I cannot be in bed in traction. I have to get up and go and do, and I have done it.

I have crawled out of the bed when I felt like I was going to die. In fact, I felt like dying would be better. Dying would have been painless compared to what I was experiencing at the time. In spite of it, I said, ''I believe I am well, so I have to get up and go.'' And while I am going is when suddenly I realize, "Hey! You know, I don't hurt anymore! Where did the pain go?!"

God said it, I must say it and that is when I get it. In Mark 11:24, Jesus says, **Therefore I say unto you, What things soever ye desire, when ye pray, believe that ye receive them, and ye shall have them.** That is a positive. He told me that I could have my desires. And if you look at the scriptures in total concerning desires, the qualifying statement would be this — and I am paraphrasing it — "I can have my desire as long as my desire is consistent with a godly life."

God's Word Ought to Produce Results

There are two ways to understand the ways of God. One is by reading and believing His Word. The second is to experience God's Word.

There should be a time, somewhere in my life, when I actually experience what God says in His Word. If His Word is true, if it is valid and if I do what He says, it has to produce a tangible result in my life, somewhere, sometime. If 100 years pass and I keep believing and confessing God's Word and never receive anything that God's Word says I should receive, then there could be some serious doubts as to whether or not it is really true. Somewhere, sometime, it ought to produce results.

By operating in the power of positive confession and observing God's Word, I have received everything that I have ever personally desired. I have always made sure that my desires were consistent with a godly life. And I always made sure that what I desired I could find a basis for it in the Word of God.

Philippians 4:19 says, **But my God shall supply all your NEED....** And there is a way you can put your needs and desires together. You cannot find in the Bible where it specifically says that God will give you a Cadillac, Mercedes

Benz, Maserrati, Rolls Royce, or a Volkswagen. But it does say He will supply your *need*.

I have a need for a vehicle so that I can be independent of public transportation and be able to go to work and come home when I want to. I could believe God for an automobile, because that is a need. He said He would supply all of my need, so that would mean a need for shelter as well as a need for transportation. But He also said, *what things soever I desire.*

Since I have a need for "wheels," why not go ahead and desire the best wheels that are rolling? Beauty is in the eye of the beholder. The Rolls Royce was the best in my opinion. So, I believed God for a Rolls Royce and He gave me one and I did not have to pay a dime for it. He gave it to me because I asked Him for it. CONFESSION WORKS!

Your Faith Will Never Rise
Above the Level of Your Confession

There is a spiritual law that says, "Your faith will never rise above the level of your confession." As you read this statement again, say it out loud and make it personal: "MY FAITH WILL NEVER RISE ABOVE THE LEVEL OF MY CONFESSION."

Again, looking at Mark 11:24, Jesus said, **Therefore, I say unto you, What things soever ye desire, when ye pray, believe that ye receive them, and ye shall have them.** Right away someone will challenge you by saying it is dishonest to say that they believe they are healed when they have pain in their body. Mentally, some people have a real problem with this concept. The reason they have a problem is that they miss one very small, but important item about Mark 11:24.

Jesus said that if you *BELIEVE* **that ye receive them, and ye shall have them.** It is obvious that you do not have it when you pray about it, because if you actually physically

34

had it when you prayed about it, then you would not have to "shall have" it later.

Understand that "shall have" is a future tense designation, indicating that the time of action has not yet taken place, but it shall, future tense.

He did not say when you pray *feel* like you are well. He said, BELIEVE IT. Again, the point I am making is if He had said "feel like it," and you still had pain, then you would be telling a lie. He did not even say when you pray, *know* it. He did not say, when you pray, *see* it. He did not say when you pray, *understand* it. He said, believe it! Believe you receive it, and then He said, *You shall have it.*

If you do not have it already, you cannot say you have it. You have to say, "I believe I have it." "I believe I have it" is a confession of faith. It is not a confession of physical fact.

So, when I am attacked with sickness, I go to the Word of God, and God says in 1 Peter 2:24, . . . **by whose stripes ye were healed.** Then I have to speak life to my life according to Proverbs 18:21, **Death and life are in the power of the tongue.**

I have to believe that what God says about me is true, because the Bible says that it is impossible for God to lie. So, if it is impossible for God to lie, the only alternative is that God must tell the truth. As a result, I must be healed whether I look like it, or whether I feel like it, or whether I see it, or whether I understand it or not. Because if I am not healed, then God is a liar.

You might think it does not make sense, but thank God a thousand times over that it does not have to make sense. Because if it had to make sense, we would all be up the creek in a boat with no oars.

I am *not* telling a lie when I say I believe I am healed. I only talk about what I believe and what I believe is based on what God says in His Word. In the natural, we do this every day of our lives and never question it. We normally give other people the benefit of the doubt and act on what they say on our behalf, and give them the chance to make it good. But when it comes to God, we want God to prove it to us first, then we will accept it.

When you go to the airport and buy a ticket to go somewhere, you do not tell the airline to "prove to me you are going to take me to New York City." You will never know until you get on the plane and arrive in New York City. You have to take them at their word. You have to act on their word.

When you begin working for a company and they say they will pay you $500 per week, they usually do not pay you the money *before* you do the work. And I guarantee you, you did not spend any time fasting and praying the first week leading up to pay day praying about whether or not the company will have enough money in the bank to pay you at the end of the week. In fact, to show you how much confidence you have in the word of those people, whom you did not even know, you go out and begin telling your friends, "See me next week, I'm going to get paid on Friday." Now that is amazing!

We know for a fact, between Monday and Friday, many companies have failed and gone into bankruptcy, filing Chapters 7, 8, 9 and 11; they had no money in the bank to pay their employees. Yet, you cannot find one time where God ever failed to honor His Word!

There are passages in the Bible which tell us that we have an adversary who is Satan. He is called the god of this world. This world that we live in is a three dimensional, physical, tangible, material world. Satan is the god who operates through the material world to get to us who are material creatures. Without realizing it, when you confess or speak the circumstances, you are opening the door and giving Satan a license to fulfill what you are saying with your mouth.

Do not misunderstand me, though, because if I am actually sick, *I am sick!!* Because if I were not actually sick, I would not need to be healed anyway, would I? So God is acknowledging that there is sickness and disease because He said, *With Jesus' stripes you were healed.* How could you be healed of something that does not exist? The very fact that you were healed with Jesus' stripes indicates the reality of sickness and disease. Do you understand that?

When God said *With Jesus' stripes you were healed,* when He said, *Lay hands on the sick and they shall recover,* they must need recovering from something.

What Makes God's Power Work?

What makes God's power work is not for us to talk or confess circumstances (what we see, what we feel, and what we are experiencing), but rather, confess God's remedy, God's cure for the situation. That is what changes the situation, and that is what faith is all about.

When I say what God says, I am not telling a lie. If I have pain and I say I do not have pain, I lied. I am a liar. But if I say, "I believe I am healed," even though I have a temperature of 105, even though I HURT, I am not telling a lie, because I am not talking about how I feel. If I said I did not hurt when, in fact, I did hurt, I would be telling a lie.

If I prayed three days ago according to Mark 11:24 and I believed that I received my healing, I must now say, "I believe that I *am* healed."

Remember that Hebrews 11:1, says **Now faith is....** I have to keep it in the present tense. At that point I will be speaking life to my life. So, I will be making a positive confession based on God's Word.

So What If People Think You Are Strange!

It takes time to program yourself to confess God's Word instead of the circumstances, but the rewards and the benefits are astounding. You have nothing to lose but your negative situation.

If what I have been talking about did not work, and you said, "I believe I'm healed" when you were sick, you would not be any worse off, because you are *still* sick and you *still* hurt, so you might as well say it: "Praise God, I believe I'm healed!"

As I told you before, twenty years ago, I began finding out what God said about me, and I began confessing what He said about me. And since God cannot lie, I began to say, "That's me! Praise God I'm blessed going out and blessed coming in. I'm the head and not the tail. I'm blessed in the city and blessed in the field. I believe I'm healed from the top of my head to the soles of my feet. I believe all my needs are met according to His riches in glory by Christ Jesus!

The reason you have to say it is because there is a divine law in Romans 10:17 that says, **So then faith cometh by hearing, and hearing by the word of God.** I do not know about you, but I have more confidence in my word than I do in anyone else's. I know my word is good! I absolutely, positively know it.

What is the point I am making? The point is that if I say "I believe I'm healed," do you know I just heard me say that?! And if I have confidence in anyone's word, I ought to have confidence in mine. So, every time I say it, I hear it and every time I hear it, it is reinforcing my faith on that subject, so I have to say it out loud.

Right away, someone might say, "But, but, but, what are people gonna think if they hear me say that?" Well, that is the bottom line, you have to make a decision as to who you are going to please — people or GOD?! Yes, people will think you are strange, but they will think you are strange while you are filing for bankruptcy, so they might as well think you are strange for doing something that is going to benefit you. And besides that, you cannot control what people think.

No matter what you do, everyone will not always think you are right. Someone will think you are a crook anyway. If you worry about what people think, you will be in trouble for sure. You have to think about you and the Lord. You have to begin to say it, confess it.

Remember, YOUR FAITH WILL NEVER RISE ABOVE THE LEVEL OF YOUR CONFESSION.

4
And God Said....

I know that I quote Mark 11:24 a lot and refer to it often, but that is because it is such an important principle for the Body of Christ to know. But I want you to see that this biblical principle is enunciated in other places as well.

1 John 5:14,15:

And this is the confidence that we have in him, that, if we ask any thing according to his will (doesn't "ask *anything*" sound something like what things *soever?*), **he heareth us** (or hears us),

And if we know that he hear us (or hears us), **whatsoever we ask,** (whatsoever sounds like *anything*, sounds like *what things soever*), **we know that we have the petitions that we desired of him.**

Notice what it does not say. It does not say *we know that we are going to get it.* It says, we know that *we have!* You might say, "But I don't see it." That is why you have faith. Because according to Hebrews 11:1, **faith is the evidence of things not seen.** "But I can't believe that I have something that I can't see." Have you ever seen your brain? You say you have brains... prove it! Let us *see* it! Let me see your brain. How do you know you have a brain? You have been told that all your life, but you were told a lot of other things all your life and found out later that they were not true. Like the fat cat in the red suit coming down the chimney flying through the sky with reindeer, bringing Christmas gifts. So how do you know you have a brain?

Maybe they have been lying to us all the time. Do you have lungs? Have you ever seen your lungs? How do you

41

know that you have a pituitary gland? Do you have veins and arteries in your body? How do you *know*? Have you seen them? Have you ever seen your spinal cord? No! But somebody told you that you have one and you believe it.

Verse 15 again, **And if we know....** What does know mean? It means a foregone conclusion. It is absolute. There is no debate, no argument. First John 5:15 says, **And if we know that he hear us, whatsoever we ask, we know that we have the petitions that we desired of him.** If God says I have it, then I have it. I cannot stress that enough. IF GOD SAYS I HAVE IT, THEN, I HAVE IT!

What I have to do is begin to speak life to my life. Begin to speak what God says. When I pray, He says ...**if I ask any thing according to his will...** *Any thing.* That would include healing, my needs met, it would include everything. I have to believe I have it because He said in the Bible that I do. He said, **And if we know that he hear us, whatsoever we ask, we know that we have the petitions....** *We have it.* How? We have it by *faith!*

God Wants Us to Copy Him

So by faith we say, "Praise God, I believe my need is met. Praise God, I believe I am healed. Praise God, I believe. I believe. I believe...whatever it is. You have to begin to say that, and begin to see yourself with it. Begin to take God at His Word, and when you do that, you will be the recipient of the thing your heart desires.

Why is it that God wants us to say things with our mouths? He wants us to pattern ourselves after Him because everything He ever did, He did it with His *mouth.* He did it by words.

Go back and read the first chapter of Genesis. Throughout that chapter, you will continually read where it says, AND GOD SAID, AND GOD SAID, AND GOD SAID. If you are very astute and observant about your reading, you will notice that nothing came into being in that chapter until after God said it. That is very interesting.

Natural human rationale would say, "All right, God is God, He is a Super Being. He has Supernatural abilities. All He has to do is wave His hand and things will come to pass. Snap His fingers, and boom, there would be the dry land! Zap! There would be the stars." But it is interesting that the Bible records that God prefaced all of his actions by *words*. That is strange. AND GOD SAID, LET THERE BE LIGHT, *and behold, there was light,* but not until *after* God said it.

Why did He record it in the Bible? Because He wants the children to act like the parents. And you know, that is what they do. Kids act like their parents, especially if they have a relatively good home situation where the father and mother are both in the home. Kids will emulate their parents. That is really their first example that they have.

God wants us to copy Him. God is a talker. God is a "sayer." God said, LET THERE BE. . . And that is what He wants us to do. LET THERE BE. . . . Be what?! "Divine health in my body." LET THERE BE. . . . Be what?! "No sickness or disease in my body." Well, begin to *say* it!!

Another reason that God requires us to confess not what we *feel*, not what we *see*, not what we *understand*, but what His Word says, is because our faith, as I said before, will never rise above the level of our confession.

Satan is a squatter. . .He will set up
housekeeping right in the empty void in your life.

Think about it, if you are not saying anything, you will not get anything. When you do not say it (what God says), then you create a void and that is when Satan moves in. Satan is a squatter who will move right in and take over.

He will set up housekeeping right in that empty void of your life. That is why you *must* say it and you have to say it all the time.

It has to become a habit with you. You have to train yourself, discipline yourself to say it. In the natural, sometimes I get tired of *saying*, "I believe I am healed," but I do not get tired of *being* healed, so I keep on saying it. I got more tired of being sick, so I found out that if I say it, that helps to promote the manifestation of my heart's desires.

Please note, THE CONFESSION OF WHAT GOD SAYS IN HIS WORD IS MY FAITH SPEAKING, AND THAT IS WHAT CAUSES IT TO COME TO PASS OR BE PHYSICALLY MANIFESTED IN MY LIFE. That is what makes it work.

You have to be a talker. Some people say, "I don't like to talk." Then go without!

In all situations, we must always remember that our confession must be based on what God says in His WORD. You may say, "Does that mean that I cannot have any thoughts of my own, that God doesn't want me to think on my own?" No! It could not mean that, because that is why He gave you that head full of sand — otherwise, called a brain! He *wants* you to think. But bring your thinking into line with God's thinking. You still put it into your own words, but it will be *God's principles.* And what is wrong with that? Because you do that all the time anyway.

You do the things you see in the movies, on television, things you hear in songs. Many of the words and phrases that some of you use, you picked up by listening to the radio. You heard something that sounded good and you began adopting that into your own life. And that is all right, as long as it is *good.*

Some people want to be original about everything. I do not care about being original. If I come up with something original, that is well and good, but if I do not,

I am not going to go without. I will use *yours* if it is not nailed down! I do not have a problem with it. But with some people, if they did not invent it, or think of it, then, it is no good.

Another biblical example is found in Exodus 15:26 where it states,

> **And said, If thou wilt diligently hearken to the voice of the Lord thy God, and wilt do that which is right in his sight, and wilt give ear to his commandments, and keep all his statutes, I will put none of these diseases upon thee, which I have brought upon the Egyptians: for I am the Lord that healeth thee.**

Unfortunately, when this was translated from the original Hebrew into English, every word was not always translated to its fullest extent. Why? I do not know.

Dr. Robert Young, a Hebrew and Greek scholar, who also wrote *Young's Concordance,* tells us that Exodus 15:26 (and many other verses) have been translated in the "causative sense" instead of the "permissive sense" as they should have been. It is obvious from the Bible, and even human history, that God does not *cause* sickness and disease, but He does permit it.

Exodus 15:26 should be translated thusly:

> **And said, If thou wilt diligently hearken to the voice of the Lord thy God, and wilt do that which is right in his sight, and wilt give ear to his commandments, and keep all his statutes, I will *permit* none of these diseases upon thee, which I have *permitted* upon the Egyptians: for** (or because) **I am the Lord that healeth thee.**

If God is the Lord that healeth thee, He cannot at the same time be the Lord that maketh thee sick. He would be working at cross purposes with Himself. Not only that, but the Bible tells us in James 1:17 that:

> Every *good* gift and every *perfect* gift is from above, and cometh down from the Father of lights, with whom is no variableness, neither shadow of turning.

Since every good and perfect gift comes down from God, sickness could not come from above, because there is nothing good or perfect about sickness and disease, and I certainly would not call it a gift. Would you?

As another example of what we can and should confess:

Psalm 103:2,3:

> Bless the Lord, O my soul, and forget not all his benefits:
>
> Who forgiveth all thine iniquities; who healeth all thy diseases.

What I have learned to do where it says, "thy," is to put my name in there. In other words: Who healeth all *Fred's* diseases. He is talking to me. This is for *me*. This is for Fred. So I say, "Praise God, thank You, Father, for healing all my diseases. Who forgiveth all *Fred's* iniquities, who healeth all *Fred's* diseases."

I have to believe that, and I have to confess it, if I ever expect to have it manifested in my daily life.

Isaiah 53:1-5 says:

> Who hath believed our report? and to whom is the arm of the Lord revealed?
>
> For he shall grow up before him as a tender plant, and as a root out of a dry ground: he hath no form nor comeliness; and when we shall see him, there is no beauty that we should desire him.
>
> He is despised and rejected of men; a man of sorrows, and acquainted with grief: and we hid as it were our faces from him; he was despised, and we esteemed him not.

Surely he hath borne our griefs, and carried our sorrows: yet we did esteem him stricken, smitten of God, and afflicted.

But he was wounded for our transgressions, he was bruised for our (Fred's) iniquities: the chastisement of our (Fred's) peace was upon him; and with his stripes we are healed.

You have to see that personally! Notice Verse Five: But He was wounded for *our* transgressions, He was bruised for *our* iniquities: the chastisement of our peace was upon Him; and with His stripes *we are* healed.

Do you realize that in every one of those four designations, it is clear that the reason why He took those things is so that we would not have to. God is not a masochist. He does not want both His own Son and us to pay for the same crime *twice!* Even in the natural world, people do not believe in paying for the same thing twice.

It says that He was wounded for our transgressions. *Not* for *His* — but for *ours!* Why would He be wounded for ours? So that we would not have to be. He was bruised for our iniquities. He did it on our behalf. The chastisement of our peace was upon Him so that we would not have to be chastised, and with His stripes, we are healed.

If we are healed, then we are not sick. Because we cannot be healed and sick at the same time. You are one or the other. The reason you need to be healed is because you are sick. But if you are sick and you get healed, the reason you get healed is so that you won't be sick anymore. If you have healing, you do not have sickness. If you have sickness, you do not have healing. You have one or the other. You either have light or dark. You cannot have both of them at the same point in time and space. It is impossible.

In Matthew's Gospel, we have the fulfillment of Isaiah 53.

Matthew 8:16,17:

> When the even was come, they brought unto him many that were possessed with devils: and he cast out the spirits with his word, and healed all that were sick:

> That it might be fulfilled which was spoken by Esaias (or Isaiah) the prophet, saying, Himself took our infirmities, and bare our sicknesses.

Based upon that, my confession is, "Praise God, thank You, Father, that Himself took my infirmities and bore my sicknesses."

Notice here, it says, Himself took... The word *took* is a past tense designation. If it had said Himself *will take,* that would be what? Future tense.

If it said, Himself *is taking,* that would be present tense. But it says, *Himself took....* That is past tense. So, you see, in the mind of God, He has already done it! As a result, I say, again, "Praise God! Father, I thank You that Jesus took all my infirmities." If He took them *all,* I do not have *any.* So, I confess I am free! I have no infirmities.

We Do Not Have To Accept Sickness and Disease

Satan has no legal right to put sickness and infirmities on us. We do not have to accept sickness and disease. I realize that this is a "bomb," and I know some people cannot handle it. People get upset when you say that you do not have to be sick. But do not worry about it. Go ahead and be sick. We do not need to argue about it. You can be sick if you want to, it is still open to you.

You can be just as sick as you want to be. In fact, you can get so sick you can die from it. It is *your* choice. But do not begrudge me. If I want to delude myself and deceive myself into thinking I can be well, so what? I am giving God all the glory. You are sick and dying and giving God the glory. I believe I am well, and I am supposed to be well, and I will always be well, and I am giving God glory. So, what is the problem?!

Another illustration is James 5:14,15:

> **Is any sick among you? let him call for the elders of the church; and let them pray over him, (FOR WHAT?) anointing him with oil in the name of the Lord: (FOR WHAT?)**
>
> **And the prayer of faith shall SAVE the sick, and the Lord shall raise him up; and if he have committed sins, they shall be forgiven him.**

Any sick refers to *anybody* — male, female, man, woman, boy, girl, black, white, brown, red, yellow, old, young, rich, poor, educated, uneducated, apartment dweller, single family residence dweller, camper dweller, trailer court dweller — ANYBODY! Let him call for the elders of the church and let them pray over him anointing him with oil in the name of the Lord: and the prayer of faith shall save the sick. *That* is the key — the prayer of faith!

You do not have to anoint with oil, but you can. It is just one of the many ways God has made available for us to be healed. God wants us well to such an extent that He has not limited Himself to just one channel by which He can bring healing to us, but He has a variety of ways. No matter where your faith is, there is a way to reach you. That is what is exciting to me.

What is the oil for? As a point of contact through which God can move. See, some of us are so earthly bound and so physically oriented that it takes something tangible for us to release our faith, so God accommodates us. He comes down on our level. The oil is not anointed. The oil is not what is important. It is the *faith*.

It is the PRAYER OF FAITH that shall heal the sick. It did not say the oil would. Faith does, not the oil. Thank God, the prayer of faith shall save the sick, so I have to believe that and *say* it, if it is to work for me.

First Peter 2:24 is a very familiar scripture, but again, it is just an example of the kind of things that we need to learn how to speak to our lives.

Who his own self bare our sins in his own body on the tree, that we, being dead to sins, should live unto righteousness: by whose stripes ye were healed.

If that is not God's will, what is it? I have heard some say, "That scripture is not talking about physical healing, Brother Price. It is talking about spiritual healing." That sounds plausible, but it is not tenable relative to the Word of God, because nowhere in the Bible, from Genesis to Revelation, does it ever tell us or even *suggest* that God heals *sick spirits.*

When Jesus walked this earth, He said, **he that hath seen me, hath seen the Father** (John 14:9). No, He did not mean that the Father looked like Jesus physically, but what He meant was that when you see Him in actions and hear His Words, you are seeing the Father. He said, **I came not to do my will, but the will of Him that sent me.** In fact, He went so far as to say, it is not even me doing the works, **it is the Father in me, he doeth the works.**

If healing were for the spirit of man and not for the physical body of man, then somewhere along the line, it seems like God would have helped us out by giving us at least one example of it. You do not find one place anywhere in the four Gospels where He, or His disciples, healed somebody spiritually. Leprosy is not a spiritual thing, it manifests itself in the human flesh. Deafness is not something that is in the spirit. It is physical bodies that go deaf. It is not lame spirits, but it is lame physical bodies that need restoring.

In reference to 1 Peter 2:24 again, **Who his own self bare our sins in his own body....** Understand that sin has to do with the spirit and the spiritual relationship with God. That is understandable and that is understood by the Word of God. But, what is He saying? The results of sin are manifested in the physical body.

At the pool of Bethesda, Jesus found the man who had a condition for 38 years. He said, "Wilt thou be made whole?" to the man, and the man answered, "I have no one to put me in the water when the waters are troubled." And Jesus looked at him and said, "Rise, take up your bed and go to your house," and the man was instantly healed. Jesus conveyed himself away, according to the scripture, into the crowd. Later on, Jesus met up with the man again. And what did Jesus say to the man? He said, "Sin no more lest a worse thing come on thee."

What was wrong with the man? He was lame and could not walk. He was a paralytic. So Jesus said, "Do not sin anymore lest something worse comes on you." Worse what? Worse physically. You could be deaf, dumb, blind, and lame. That would be worse than just being lame.

So, with His stripes ye were healed. *Were* is past tense, and if ye *were*, ye *are*, and if ye *are*, ye *is*. I like to say it that way. I know it is not good English, but it helps me to understand it more clearly. That means I am healed RIGHT NOW. And I believe that I am healed. I am speaking life to my life.

When sickness and disease try to assault my body, I stand toe to toe and eyeball to eyeball, and nose to nose with it, and I say to the sickness and disease monster that comes against me: "You foul spirit, you are defeated. You are whipped. I am healed in the name of Jesus. Back off! Get away from me. You are trespassing on Holy ground."

You have to *say* it if you want God's power to work for you! "Yes, but that sounds strange." I do not care how it sounds. I am not interested in how it sounds. I am interested in results. "But people might think you're not very smart saying that." Who cares what people think?! I am only concerned about what God thinks. That is all. That

51

is where help is coming from. Help is not coming from folk. All you will get from most people is criticism, misunderstanding, false accusations, jealousy, pride, envy and strife. That will not help me or you.

Some of you are having a problem understanding this principle and you say, ''But I don't understand how I can maintain a positive confession of healing when I don't feel healed. I don't understand, Brother Price. Wouldn't I be telling a lie? Wouldn't I be lying about it if I said I believe I am healed and my temperature is 105 and I'm aching all over?''

Many people have a problem saying, ''I believe I am healed,'' based on the Word of God written in the Covenant. Yet a person can go into the hospital having been diagnosed with some debilitating problem in their body. They can be remanded over to surgery, because the doctor has told them that there is a malignant tumor. ''We believe that based upon its size and location that we can successfully remove it in its entirety and that you can — all other things being equal — continue to lead a normal and fulfilling life.''

You Trust the Doctor's Word, Why Not Dr. Jesus' Word!

Based upon what the doctors say, the person goes into the hospital for surgery. The doctor performs a 5-1/2-hour operation on them. He cuts them open, reaches into their abdominal cavity and removes the tumor, sews them up and sends them up to the recovery room. They go through the recovery room and are finally placed on a ward. They are under intensive care for a while because they are in such bad shape. Their body has to have time to recover.

The person is watched and their vital signs are monitored. The doctor comes in, examines them and a few days later, they are in a private room. Their friends, relatives, husband or wife, and children come to see them while they are lying in bed. The patient does not look too good. They look like somebody who has gone through a traumatic experience, and they have. It has been a shock to their system to be cut open like that.

When the friends come into the room, they say, "Well, how are you doing?" And the patient answers, "Oh, I'm doing just fine. They got it all out. The doctor said I'll be going home in about three weeks." Now, is that person lying? Are they telling a lie? YES, THEY ARE! THEY ARE LYING ABOUT IT. THEY ARE IN PAIN. THEY ARE BEING GIVEN PAIN PILLS OR SHOTS EVERY HALF HOUR! There is soreness where that incision was made, where those tubes have been injected into the body.

The person does not feel well. They do not feel good. They do not feel like everything is all right, but they are saying, "I'm all right, they got it all out." Why? THE DOCTOR SAID SO. THEY SAID THEY GOT IT ALL OUT.

You did not see the tumor being taken out. You did not see, with your own eyes, the operation being performed. You were under anesthesia. You do not know what they took out. They may have put something *in* instead of taking something out. But you are taking the word of the doctor!

You have trusted your life into the hands of this man who is supposed to be a medical professional, and he says you are all right. "We got it all out. There is no more malignancy in your body." Nevertheless, you are still in pain. You are still hurting. You are still physically not quite right. Your head is rocking and reeling from the medication and the anesthesia and drugs. But you are *telling everybody,* "I'm all right. I'm going back to work in about 30 days. I'll be home in about three weeks." Why? BECAUSE THE DOCTOR SAID SO! Well, *so did doctor Jesus!*

So, why are you having such a problem saying, "I believe I'm healed? With His stripes I was. I believe I'm well."

If it is okay for you to say that you are all right because the doctor said so, yet you are still in pain, your body is not well yet, but you are confessing what the doctor said. . . . Are you lying? No, you are basing your information on the word of someone you have respect for. Someone you feel knows what they are talking about, a medically trained professional person.

Likewise, what is wrong with me saying, "I believe I'm healed?" I have the test results from the laboratory. It said, "With His stripes I was healed." Yes, I have pain in my body. Yes, I still have the incision where the operation was performed, but the Master got it all out! I believe I am well.

So, what is the big problem?! Why am I lying when I say what God says, but telling the truth when I say what the doctor says? We trust the word of man and make confessions based upon what they tell us. Why will we not trust the Word of the Chief Resident Surgeon of all the ages? Hallelujah! I rest my case.

A negative confession nullifies His Word
on our behalf.

Read the next statement very carefully — it is of supreme importance:

God clearly tells us what He will do for us in His Word and from that point on, He deals with us on the basis of what we confess and do about His promises. A negative confession nullifies His Word on our behalf.

That is awesome! That is why He gave us His Word, because without His Word, there would be no way we could ever exercise faith to believe His Word. You cannot exercise faith in a vacuum. There has to be some object to set your faith on. In the case of God, it is His Word.

That is why Satan works so tenaciously to keep the Word of God out of the hands of the people, because he knows if they ever learn how to confess that Word, they will open the flood gates for God to move on their behalf, and his season of dominating their lives will be over. No slaveholder likes to lose his slaves.

In Mark 16:19,20, we see the importance of God's Word:

> So then after the Lord had spoken unto them, he was received up into heaven, and sat on the right hand of God.
>
> And they went forth, and preached every where, the Lord working with them, and *confirming the word* with signs following.

Notice that it did not say He confirmed *them,* but *He confirmed His Word.* If there is no Word, God has nothing to confirm.

5

Out of the Abundance of the Heart the Mouth Speaketh

To show how important our words are, Jesus says in Matthew 12:34:

> **O generation of vipers, how can ye, being evil, speak good things? for out of the abundance of the heart the mouth speaketh.**

That is awesome! *Death* and *life* are in the power of the *tongue*. Your heart is your spirit. That is the part of you that has been born again.

Jesus did not say, . . . out of the abundance of the head. That is where we have missed it. We have been thinking we had to deal with God scientifically or academically. No! Jesus said, for out of the abundance of the heart, the mouth speaks.

Whatever is in your heart in abundance, that is what is going to come out of your mouth, and that, my dear, precious friend, is what is going to control your life!

What do you have down there in your heart in abundance? Abundance means a *whole lot*. It means *"mucho"* or *much*. For out of the abundance of the heart the mouth speaks. In other words, my mouth cannot speak but what is in my heart. What is in there in abundance? What have you been programming into your heart in abundance?

Many have been born again. No question about it, their names are written in the Lamb's Book of Life. They are children of God. If they were to die today, they would go to heaven, no question about it. But what about *this* life?

If all God wanted you to do was go to heaven, then the most natural thing that should happen as soon as you confess Christ as your personal Savior, is that you ought to drop dead so you can go right on to heaven. There is no point in hanging around here for 60 more years! What for? What are you going to do down here for 60 more years if God's plan is for you to go to heaven?

No, God's plan is for you to live here victoriously. Then, when you finish here, take a vacation and go on to heaven, because that is when you will be at rest. You will be sunning yourself on God's beaches. But now, He wants us to live down here.

Jesus said, **I came....** He did not say, I drew you up to heaven. He said, **I came that you might have life and have it more abundantly.** He wants us to have abundant life. Not struggling. Not hard trials and tribulations. Not trying to claw your way up the back side of the mountain.

He said, "I came that you might have life and have it more abundantly." But we will never experience that abundant life until we learn how to operate in the spiritual law of the power of positive confession.

Matthew 12:34b-37:

> ...for out of the abundance of the heart the mouth **speaketh.**
>
> **A good man out of the good treasure of the heart bringeth forth good things: and an evil man out of the evil treasure bringeth forth evil things.**
>
> **But I say unto you, That every idle word that men shall speak, they shall give account thereof in the day of judgment.**
>
> **For by thy words thou shalt be justified, and by thy words thou shalt be condemned.**

Notice what that verse does not say. It does not say, for by thy *works* thou shalt be justified and by thy *works* thou shalt be condemned. No, He said, **By thy** *words.* By the words of *your* mouth. That is awesome!

By your works, you will get some rewards, or lose rewards if the works are not the works of God. He said, by your words, you will be justified. *Justified* means "declared righteous." That is how you got saved, by your mouth.

Romans 10:9,10:

That if thou shalt CONFESS with thy MOUTH the Lord Jesus, and shalt believe in thine heart that God hath raised him from the dead, thou shalt be saved.

For with the heart man believeth unto righteousness; and with the MOUTH *confession* **is made unto salvation.**

Change Your Mouth!

Death and life are in the power of the tongue. For out of the abundance of the heart, the mouth speaketh.

I have to let God's Word come out of my mouth to give God something to confirm in my life. If you do not like what has been happening in your life, then change your mouth! And, of course, your heart. Change your mouth!

Do not blame the white folks, and do not blame the blacks in the ghetto. They are not your problem. Do not blame the Communists over in another country, and do not blame the moon men or the Martians. Go look in the mirror when you are in the bathroom by yourself and the door is locked. The person you see in the mirror, that is your problem.

I do not know about you, but I am thrilled to find out that nobody can mess me up. I like that. Thank God, I am the one who decides. Not because it is me, but because God designed the system to work that way. For by thy words... Jesus said. Not by *their* words.

What you say does not make any difference. Not when it comes to me and my personal life and relationship with

God. Thank God, I am the only one who can mess that up. My wife cannot mess it up. My kids cannot mess it up — not my personal, individual life. When we do something corporately as a family, then they can hinder me. If we do something corporately as a church, then they can hinder me. But I can step out of that role and get over here in my own thing and the Lord and I can go for it! And I like that.

We cannot blame anyone else. If I mess up, that is me. I have to go ahead and admit, "I am the one who messed up." Some people are always giving alibis. "Well, if it wasn't for *those folk* down there; if it wasn't for the people over there; if it wasn't for the Democrats; if it wasn't for the Republicans." TAKE THE RESPONSIBILITY YOURSELF! *YOU* ARE THE ONE! IT'S NOBODY ELSE'S FAULT.

It has nothing to do with where you were born. It has nothing to do with your mother, your father, your sister or your brother. It has nothing to do with anything but you and God, and you ought to thank God on a daily basis that that is the case. Thank Him that nobody can mess you up. If you are messed up, it is your own fault and not God's. You cannot blame anyone else, because you can climb out of that pit!

I do not want to hear about how bad you had it. "Well, you just don't know how abused I was when I was a kid." But you are not a kid *now*. What is your excuse now? Besides that, that abuse is under the blood of Jesus and that blood will cleanse that abuse. If you will do what His Word says, **Casting all your care on him; for he careth for you** (1 Pet. 5:7), then it will not rise up to threaten you or be a specter in the dark of night to frighten you while you are in your bed alone.

I do not care what *they* did. They could have raped you, beat you on the head and done everything they wanted to do to you. That has nothing to do with the blood of Jesus. It has nothing to do with the fact that you are a child of

God *right now.* Stop copping out with all that junk of the past! It means nothing. It is over. It is done!

No, it should not have happened. No, your father should not have molested you, but he did. It is over. Forget it, and go forward. Stop living in the past. It will do you no good.

Philippians 3:13,14:

...Forgetting those things which are behind, and reaching forth unto those things which are before,

I press toward the mark for the prize of the high calling of God in Christ Jesus.

What happened to you should never have happened. They should not have done that, but they did, and your thinking about it and carrying it to your grave is not going to change it. Put it under your feet. Bury that garbage. Forget it and get a hold of the Word of God.

Let the Word get down in your heart so that there is an abundance there, so that when you open your mouth, out comes the Word of God and then He will confirm that in your life.

Yes, your first marriage was a disaster, but so what! It is over! You made a mistake. Forget about it. Go on to something else.

You may say, "I don't have any confidence in men. I don't trust men. They are all alike." You are lying! I rebuke that. All men are not alike. Just because you got a hold of a rat, do not think every man is a rat! "Men ain't no good. Honey, don't trust no man!" I have news for you. It was a man Who redeemed you. Better watch your mouth!

It is a Man sitting at the right hand of God interceding on your behalf. It is a Man Who loved you. It is a Man Who exalted you to a station of life that has respect, and it is a Man Who is coming back to receive you to Himself. WATCH YOUR MOUTH!

Put your past behind you and start letting the Word of God come out of your mouth. Hide it down in your heart. God will confirm it in your life. Nobody and nothing can stop you!

Circumstances cannot do a thing to me
without my consent.

I want to ask you a question: *Who do you think determines whether or not you can have the abundant life of health, prosperity, joy, victory, and fruitfulness which Jesus promised?*

Most people would answer, "God." But human experience does not bear that out. Some Christians are well and others are sick. Some have abundance while others struggle economically and materially. Some die young and are cut off in the prime of life, while others live out a long and full life. No, it could not be God.

Could it be Satan, better known as the devil?

James 4:7 says,

Submit yourselves therefore to God. Resist the devil, and he will flee from you.

How do you submit yourself to God? By submitting yourself to His Word. For God and His Word are one. When you submit to God's Word, you are submitting to God. According to God's Word, we can resist the devil and he *must* flee from us. That being true, then the devil could have nothing at all to do with whether we succeed or fail, live in wealth or lack. If not the devil, *who?!*

I repeat the question: *Who do you think determines whether or not you enjoy the full rich life of health and peace and prosperity that God promised in His Word?*

The scriptures tell us it is not God or the devil. Then who could it be? Could it be circumstances? Whatever will be, will be. Maybe it is circumstances? No! *Circumstances merely give you the opportunity to reveal the extent of your faith in God's Word.* Circumstances cannot do a thing to me without my consent. Circumstances in and of themselves cannot cause victory or defeat. It is my response to the circumstances that determines what influence they will have on my life.

Matthew 17:20 gives us insight into this principle:

And Jesus said unto them, Because of your unbelief: for verily I say unto you, If ye have faith as a grain of mustard seed, ye shall say unto this mountain, Remove hence to yonder place; and it shall remove; and nothing shall be impossible unto you.

Jesus said that. Is He a liar?

There was a man who brought his demonized child to the disciples and the disciples did not cast out the demon. Jesus was on the Mount of Transfiguration. When He came on the scene, He cast the demon out. After the man and his boy left, the disciples came to Him and asked, ''Why could not we cast him out?'' And Jesus said, in essence, that it was not the circumstances, but, rather, *Because of your unbelief.*

In Matthew 17:14-16, we learn something very important:

And when they were come to the multitude, there came to him a certain man, kneeling down to him, and saying, Lord, have mercy on my son: for he is lunatic, and sore vexed: for ofttimes he falleth into the fire, and oft into the water. And I brought him (Who brought him? The father.) **to thy disciples, and they could not cure him.**

The man said they *could not* cure him — meaning either they did not have the power or the authority to do it. If that is true, then the father was a fool. For why would you bring your child to someone who had no power or ability to cure him? The problem was, the man's interpretation of the circumstances of the situation was invalid. He said they *could not,* when literally, what he should have said was that they *did not.*

There *had* to be something in that man's experience that indicated that these disciples could help him; otherwise, he was foolish to bring his child to someone that he did not have any faith in. He had either heard about or seen the disciples do something, and it had inspired him to believe that they could help his child. For some reason, it did not work. So the father's interpretation was that they *could not.*

But there is a difference between *could* not and *did* not. Jesus answered and said,

> . . . O faithless and (O what? FAITHLESS! Do you know what faithless means? It means less faith.) perverse generation, how long shall I be with you? how long shall I suffer you? (or put up with you) bring him hither to me. And Jesus rebuked the devil (or literally the demon); and he departed out of him: and the child was cured from that very hour.
>
> Then came the disciples to Jesus apart, and said, *Why could not we cast him out?*
>
> **Matthew 17:17-19**

There is a revelation here. If they did not have either the authority of the ability to cast that demon out, would they have known that?

I would never ask the question, "Why could not I get pregnant and have a child?" I know why. I am not supposed to. I am not constructed that way. I could not if I wanted to, so I would never ask the question.

When they said, "Why could not we cast him out?" that very question indicated that they knew they had the authority and the ability, but for some reason, it did not work this time and so they said, "Why could not we do it?" If they had not been given the authority and the power or ability to do it, would they not have known that?

The point I am making here is that you can have the authority and you can have the ability and still botch it up. So just because certain things have not been happening in your life as a Christian, do not assume by that, that it *could not* have happened in your life.

Just because you are not well, just because you are not abundantly supplied, do not assume you *cannot* be or that it is not the will of God for you to have it simply because you have not been experiencing it. Maybe the problem is *you*. Just like it was the disciples.

Jesus did not say, *because you do not have the authority;* He did not say, *because you don't have the ability.* He said, *Because of your unbelief.* Even though you have been delegated the authority and the ability, you can still operate in unbelief.

Let me show you the scripture that proves they had the authority. That is why the father brought his son to them.

Matthew 10:1:

And when he had called unto him his twelve disciples, he gave them power (in the Greek, the word "power" is *exousia,* which literally means *authority)* **against unclean spirits, to cast them out....**

He gave them authority to cast them out, but they did not do it. That is the same thing that is happening to the Church today. More than 1900 years ago, Jesus Christ, the Head of the Church, gave to the Church, His Body, the authority to cast out demons; the authority to speak with new tongues; the authority to lay hands on the sick and they would recover; the authority to be victorious in life; and yet the Church has been — by and large, from a traditional point of view — whipped and defeated and not carrying out the great commission that God gave us.

We have assumed that it was not the will of God and yet, He gave the disciples that authority and He also gave it to us. But authority that is not exercised will do no one any good. All the authority does is give you the *right* to do something, but you still have to *do it*. The authority does not do it, *you* do it.

If you are not enjoying the full, rich life in Christ, do not blame God, do not blame the devil, and do not blame the circumstances. Go look in the mirror. *You* are the problem. Raise your right hand, make a finger, put it on the tip of your nose and say, *"I'm the one!"* YOU ARE THE ONE! I thank God for that, because it puts us all on par. Nobody has any advantage over anyone else.

Matthew 21:21,22:

> **Jesus answered and said unto them, Verily I say unto you, If ye have faith, and doubt not, ye shall not only do this which is done to the fig tree, but also if ye shall say unto this mountain, Be thou removed, and be thou cast into the sea; it shall be done. And all things, whatsoever ye shall ask in prayer, believing, ye shall receive.**

What You Think, Believe and Confess Preconditions Your Life

Remember this principle: *Everyone preconditions his life by what he thinks, by what he believes, and by what he confesses.* Remember what we read in Proverbs 18:21: **Death and life are in the power of the tongue....** Hebrews 3:1 says, **Wherefore, holy brethren, partakers of the heavenly calling, consider the Apostle and High Priest of our profession, Christ Jesus.**

Jesus is our High Priest. How? He is the High Priest of our *profession*. The word for profession in the Greek is actually the same word for *confession*. In other words, Jesus is the High Priest of our words. Jesus presides over our words.

As our High Priest, He can act on our behalf, to SAVE, BLESS, HEAL, PROTECT, and DELIVER — provided we give Him a positive confession which is in harmony with the Word of God. But a confession of doubt, a confession of fear concerning our circumstances and our situation in life, hinders His ministry on our behalf.

Consider this confession:

"Well, brother, sister, how are you doing today?"

"Well, I'm just *barely makin' it.*"

Or this confession:

"Well, brother, sister, how do you feel today?"

"Oh, I think I'm going to be sick."

"Well, I hear there's a very, very strong case of the flu comin' on — I'll probably get it because I always do." These kind of confessions go on all the time, and most people never think anything about it.

Jesus cannot act as the High Priest of that kind of confession, because that kind of confession is inconsistent with the Word of God. *You said*, you are probably going to be sick. *You said*, you are probably going to get the flu, and the Bible says, "With His stripes, you were healed." Did you get that? The Bible said, "With His stripes, you were healed." But you are saying you are probably going to be sick, so you cut Jesus off.

The scriptures clearly show us that sickness or health, poverty, prosperity, or adversity are directly related to our confession, to our words. A confession of doubt or fear concerning our situation or need, hinders the ministry of Jesus our High Priest on our behalf and opens a channel of access for Satan to come in like a flood to destroy and oppress.

I want to use sickness as an illustration, because that is one of the areas in which God uses me, ministering to the sick. I would like to share with you a three-fold principle.

I want you to follow this carefully, because it will not only help you individually, but it will help you to help others whom you love. It will help you to understand why some that you have known, some that you have loved, and knew that they had a genuine commitment to God and to Christ, became sick and died of that sickness.

Some people said God caused their death or illness. "The Lord took them." Others said, "God works in mysterious ways, His wonders to perform."

Most of the time, we do not know what is in the heart of another person. We really do not know what their attitude is concerning God's Word. They may be very nice people, love the Lord, and have had a genuine experience of salvation or conversion. Yet they may not know the Word of God, or they may not be committed to living it on a continuous basis. They may know it, they may have heard it, but they are not really living it. Many people are like that. Perhaps even *you!*

When illness strikes, when sickness comes, there are three things to consider if you are to receive healing. The first thing that I must know is: *What does God say about my condition?* The symptoms say, I am sick. The thermometer says I am sick. But what does God say?

Let me make this very clear, because I do not want anybody to go off and mess up on this: If the thermometer says that you have a temperature of 105, you have (in the natural) a temperature of 105. I am not denying that, but you see, you have a choice. You can either go with what the circumstance tells you, or you can go with what God tells you. Now that is an awesome choice!

Again, I do not deny that the thermometer says 105. That is not what is important to me. What is important is, what does God say about that 105 degree temperature?

You have to be absolutely, positively, unequivocally committed to the Word of God. You have to believe

WITHOUT ANY SHADOW OF DOUBT THAT WHAT GOD SAYS ABOUT YOUR CONDITION IS SO. If you have to ask the question, if you have to think, "Well what if..." forget it! Go with the thermometer. Do not waste any time, you could die. You have to be completely and totally sold out to the Word of God, and everybody is not. And that is all right. It is not a put-down. It is not meant to be condemnation.

There is a place in God where you can rise up and live in a different area than the every day, but it is going to cost you a total commitment, a sell-out. Only you can know if you are really "sold out."

Whenever you are uncertain and say things like, "What about...?" Or "Maybe..." you are not there yet, so do not play around with it. If the temperature is 105, you had better do what the doctor tells you to do to get it down from 105, because you cannot last long with a temperature of 105.

But you need to know what God says about your condition. Psalm 103:3 says:

Who forgiveth all thine iniquities; who healeth all thy diseases.

A temperature of 98.6 is considered normal. If your temperature is 105, this indicates you have a problem of some sort. Taking a stand on God's Word means you must say, "God has healed it and I now believe I receive my healing."

The thing about it is, when you make that statement, you might start feeling worse. Your temperature may go up to 106, so you have to be ready to make a stand, or else Satan will intimidate you. Every time you say, "I believe I receive..." the devil will say, "Boo!!" all designed to frighten you. But you have to be committed. You have to be sold out or it will not work. That is the point I am making.

Satan Will Try to Intimidate You

The *second* thing you need to know if you are going to

receive your healing is: "What does Satan say about my condition?" There are no Bible verses for this, but I will tell you what he says. The devil will work through your senses and through your mind. He will oppress you in the realm of the senses and then right on the heels of that, he will send a thought to your mind.

Have you ever awakened in the morning and stepped out of bed and suddenly a pain hit you in a certain part of your body? You did not go to bed with that pain. You did not dream about that pain, and you were not expecting or looking for any pain. That pain hit you maybe in the back or the leg, or an arm, or a shoulder. Then almost instantly, when you were conscious of the pain, a thought came to your mind. "You're getting arthritis, or bursitis." Or, "You are going to have a coronary."

Who do you think that came from? Do you think the Holy Ghost put that in your mind? No. That is the way Satan works. "You are going to be sick. That sharp pain you had in your breast must be cancer. After all, Grandma died from that." Now when those kinds of thoughts come, you have to be convinced that when the Word of God says, **who healeth all thy diseases,** it is talking about *you!*

Instantly you have to speak to that pain in Jesus' name. You cannot wait around. If you let fear come in, then you need to get some help fast, because you are in trouble. You have to stand against it in faith. It does not mean that you do not seek medical help to assist you in terms of the conscious awareness of the symptoms. Pain is symptomatic. Pain is not a cause of anything. It is the *result* of something. God built the body system so that it would give alerts when something goes wrong. Pain is an alert system.

If you grabbed something that was 125 degrees hot and you had no sensation in your hand, you could burn your hand off, and you would not know it. But as soon as you touch it, the alert system goes into effect. So, you may need something, perhaps medication, to deal with that conscious awareness (pain), of whatever is wrong with you, so that you can continue to function. But your faith is not in that, because that is not going to heal you anyway. The power of God will do it. Because if that medication would do it, you would never need to pray, or believe God for your healing by faith. God would have worked through the medication to do it and you would never need any divine healing.

Some people have languished on beds of affliction for years, pumped full of medications and still died from the condition. My mother-in-law, who is now deceased, is a case in point. She had acute arthritis for more than 20 years. She had taken so much medication during those 20 years that it had almost destroyed her body. She did not look like a human. She needed it to survive, and thank God for it. But if medication did it, she should have been healed after 20 years of medication. Medication has its place and it can deal with symptoms until the power of God removes the cause so that you can continue to function.

Do not let anyone put you in bondage about taking medication. Satan will tell you, "You are going to be sick. You feel that pain? That's arthritis. Remember Grandma had that. Remember, your mother-in-law died of that." If you listen to that, you begin to think that, say that, and fear comes in. That opens the door for Satan to put that on you. "Well after all, it runs in the family."

Nothing runs in *my* family but divine health. I am not accepting anything less! I do not care how often it comes, I believe I am well. In fact, I believe that I walk in divine health. That is my personal, daily confession.

What does the devil say about it? He says you are sick. What does God say about it? **Who healeth all thy diseases.** You have the choice.

The *third* thing you need to know, if you are going to receive your healing is: "What do I *say* about my condition?" There are three things you must know. (1) What does God say? (2) What does Satan say? (3) What do *you* say? Whatever *you* say is going to legitimize what God says, or what the devil says. You are the one who decides whether the battle swings to God or to the devil. YOU ARE IN CONTROL! What do you say about the condition? It is *your* choice. Your confession is what will make the difference.

Keep in mind that *you* cannot say anything if you do not know what God has already said about it in His Word. If you have not made a commitment to say what God says about it, you are in serious trouble.

Read this *very* carefully. It *could* save your life. When I said that number three is what *you* say, do not make the fatal mistake of saying what you would *like* for it to be. You must say what you actually believe in your heart. Because if not, you could die while you are waiting for what you would *like* for it to be, to come up to what you *actually are able to believe it to be.*

If you ask people, "Do you believe you are healed?" they will usually respond, "Well, I certainly *want to believe* that, Brother Price." That person *is not believing.* That is *not faith!* That is what they would like, and that is fine. They ought to want that, that ought to be their desire, but this will not work with you *wanting* that to be so, you have to *believe* it RIGHT NOW.

You do not have time to wait around while you are saying, "That is what I *would like* for it to be; that is what I would like for it to finally come to." That is not faith and that will not work and you cannot afford to gamble with your life.

The moment the symptom shows up, you have to stand on the symptom *then.* You have to pounce on it like a dog on a bone. You have to get on it like a cat with a canary and say, "I believe, according to the Word of God, that I am healed from the top of my head to the soles of my feet, to the tip of my toes, I am well in the name of Jesus." You have to do that *instantly.*

There are many of you who want the things that God has to offer, but you are not there yet, where you are able to actually say, "I believe I receive. That is it! No more discussion on the subject. I believe I am well. I believe my need is met. I believe it *now.* If you are not convinced right now, then get some help quickly. You cannot afford to wait around.

Do you understand what I am saying? You have to be convinced right now! And the way you do that, is to start using your faith on little, infinitesimal, insignificant things that do not amount to a hill of beans. Things that are not terminal. Things that are not crises. Just the little every day things that ordinarily you would not even have to use any faith on. *That* is what you practice on.

Do not wait until you have terminal cancer to PRACTICE FAITH. Do not wait until the marshal is walking up to the door to foreclose on and evict you from your house. It is too late then. Do you understand that? Do not wait until some major crisis occurs and then start saying, "I believe I receive."

This is an example of how you may begin to practice developing your faith: You may have enough money to buy a suit of clothes. Do not buy the suit of clothes with the money. Do not charge it to the charge account. Take the charge card, get the cash for the cost of the suit, and send it to a ministry. Then believe God and use your faith for that suit. If the suit never comes, it does not affect your life and you have not lost a thing. You can always go back and buy it. Do you understand that? But that is an example of how you can begin to learn to walk by faith. This is called, "on-the-job training."

What Do *You* Say About Your Condition?

What do *you* say about your condition? What you say will have to be based on what you believe, which is based on what God says in His Word.

Brother, sister, you have to be convinced. This is not a gambling situation. This is not LOTTO, a kind of "maybe you will and maybe you will not" game. This is not roulette where you throw your life on some turning wheel and hope that the right color comes up. Do not do that! You have to *know!* And if you do not know, then do something else until you do know.

Do not feel ashamed about it. You do not need to be ashamed of it. It is the wise man who recognizes his limitations and then does something about it. It is the fool who goes on, oblivious to what he is not able to do, thinking he is going to do it anyway and gets his head broken. Do not do that.

What does God say? What does the devil say? And what do *you* say? YOU are the one who decides what is going to prevail in your life. Your confession will line up with what God says, or it will line up with what the devil says. Whichever one it lines up with, guess what? That is what you are going to have in your life. If you keep up the umbrella of God's protection, you can walk right through the storm, and walk out dry! But if you do not observe to do, the curses, which are already there, will come upon you. That means you do not have an umbrella now. You have no protection. The way it is worded in verse 19, it looks like God is going to do the cursing. It should have been rendered, thus, The Lord will permit to be brought.

There are many other verses in Chapter 28 about curses, but the ones we have looked at should give you a good idea of the enormity of the curse.

Now I want to show you something else. This should help some of you who have been sitting around all your

Christian life nursing some ailment like arthritis, bursitis, heart condition, varicose veins, or whatever it might be. You have been nursing the thing, thinking you were suffering for the Lord, not realizing you were suffering because you are ignorant. Ignorant of God's Word.

Let us read Deuteronomy 28:61:

> **Also every sickness, and every plague, which is not written in the book of this law, them will the Lord** (permit to be brought) **bring upon thee until thou be destroyed.**

Verses 20-28 talk about all kinds of diseases that affect every part of your body. But then he goes on to say, God will permit to come upon you even the things that are not even written in the Book.

What am I saying? I am saying, for you who have been nursing your condition, thinking you were serving God, thinking that God wanted you to hold on and keep a stiff upper lip, and never give up and always praise Him right in the middle of all that sickness and disease, you ought to be able to tell by this that the sickness and disease were not from God. It is not the will of God!

6

Satan — Our Adversary; Jesus — Our Advocate

Revelation 12:10:

> **And I heard a loud voice saying in heaven, Now is come salvation, and strength, and the kingdom of our God, and the power of his Christ: for the accuser of our brethren is cast down, which accused them before our God day and night.**

That is why you have to be "on the job," friend. You have an adversary that works day and night. You do not stand a chance to win if you let down your guard. This opponent is out to get you. He wants you *dead!* Dead in the sense of not being able to respond through the Word of God and by the power of the Holy Spirit to be an adversary to *him.*

Think about it — he is accusing you day and night! What do you think he is accusing you with? *Words!* In other words, he is talking you down. Satan is a legalist. When it comes to us, he will use the letter of the law against us, so we need help, and God has provided that help.

God has provided a public defender who is above reproach. In fact, He has provided a public defender Who has been taught the law by the Judge. Nobody knows the law better than this public defender, and the public that He defends is the public of the Kingdom of God and that is us.

In 1 John 2:1, it says:

> **My little children, these things write I unto you,**

that ye sin not. And if any man sin, we have an advocate with the Father, Jesus Christ the righteous.

The word "advocate" is a legal term. In the Greek, this word has reference to a courtroom scene. Literally, it means *counsel for the defense.* Satan stands before the throne of God accusing the brethren day and night. The high tribunal of God is open 24 hours a day, every day of the week. There is never a holiday. It does not close down for any president's birthday. Thank God for that!

Hebrews 3:1 tells us that Jesus is the High Priest of our confession. If you combine His High Priestly function with His legal function, then He becomes the counsel for our defense, and at the same time, the High Priest of our confession.

Unlike earthly lawyers, this counsel for the defense cannot be intimidated, nor can He be bought. This counsel for the defense is not going to be concerned whether you are able to pay a fee or not. In fact, the services of this law firm are given to the citizens of this kingdom without charge. So, since there is no money involved, there cannot be any temptation involved.

How does this counsel for our defense defend us in the high tribunal of heaven when we have an adversary, the accuser of the brethren who is accusing us day and night? He defends us on the basis of two things: (1) He provides and (2) we provide. If we do not provide ours, we throw the case to the prosecuting attorney (Satan) and we will be convicted. But if we can bring our evidence, our attorney has irrefutable evidence. And by putting His evidence together with ours, it is an open and shut case in our favor, and we are set free.

Look at Revelation 12:10,11 again:

And I heard a loud voice saying in heaven, Now is come salvation, and strength, and the kingdom of our God, and the power of his Christ: for the accuser

of our brethren is cast down, which accused them before our God day and night.

And they overcame him by the blood of the Lamb, and by the word of their testimony; and they loved not their lives unto the death.

That is how Jesus defends us, on the basis of His *shed blood.* And guess what? On the word of *our* testimony! Whether you realize it or not, that word "testimony" is another word for confession.

Let me say it again: the way He defends us is on the basis of His shed blood and our confession. If I do not make a confession that is consistent with the Word of God, He does not have anything to defend me with. Can you see that? He has no defense. Then, the prosecuting attorney, the accuser of the brethren, can make the case stick against me, because I am saying what he is saying, so it looks like I am exactly what he says I am — guilty as charged. We have to learn how to say what our Father says about us so that we can bring our confession in line with His shed blood. And on the basis of His blood and our confession, we win.

Jesus is pleading our defense against Satan's accusations, not only with His precious blood, but also with our testimony, which comes right down to this, *what we say!* When I say, "I think I am going to be sick," I am not giving Him a testimony with which He can defend me, because it is contrary to the revealed law or Word of God, the statute that is on the books, so to speak. The Judge can only uphold the law which is His Word.

When I discovered this and looked back on my life, I said, "No wonder I was in court every day! No wonder I was always getting sentenced. I never said anything in line with what He could defend me with. And the churches I went to never told me that I had any defense anyway. In fact, they told me God was my problem. I did not realize that I had a prosecuting attorney who was trying to put me behind bars for life. But thank God I have an Advocate, but

I have to give Him my words. Words that are consistent with the law. God's Word, in other words. When I do that, He will defend me. If you join your confession with the confession or the words of your adversary, then Jesus cannot act as your High Priest. You tie His hands.

If an attorney, such as a public defender, has a client and the client gets in court and says, "I'm guilty, I'm guilty. I killed him. I shot him six times right between the eyes!" there is not much the attorney can do to defend that client. Likewise, when we make a confession that is inconsistent with the revealed Word of God, it is like saying, "I killed him, I killed him!" We negate our counsel for the defense's ability to defend us.

7

Affirming Four Biblical Facts Can Result in Victorious Christian Living

Let us now consider some important biblical principles, which can determine how victorious you will be in your Christian walk. The victorious Christian life is based upon a positive confession of four basic biblical facts or truths. A positive affirmation of these four facts will compel Satan to acknowledge our authority and our victory over him. This will in turn break the enemy's power to successfully bind, hinder, and oppress.

What does God expect me to confess? We must confess:

(1) WHAT WE ARE IN CHRIST.

(2) WHERE WE ARE IN CHRIST.

(3) WHAT WE POSSESS IN CHRIST.

(4) WHAT WE CAN DO IN CHRIST.

If you get a picture, a revelation of these four things, you are on your way to the top. You are on your way to victorious Christian living. You are on your way to living the kind of life that Christ gave His life for.

Christ did not give up His life for you to be whipped. He did not give up His life for you to be walked on like a doormat. Christ did not come down here and defeat death, hell, the grave, Satan, and every demon for you to be laid up on some bed of affliction for 25 years. That was not why He came. He could have remained in heaven and you would have still had that. Although the vast majority of Christians are experiencing that whipped and defeated lifestyle, and because God does not reach down supernaturally and change it, they think that must be the will of God. They fail to realize, because they have never been taught, that it is not up to God, it is up to us, whether we live defeated or victorious.

In Matthew 18:18, Jesus says,

Verily I say unto you, Whatsoever ye shall bind on earth shall be bound in heaven: and whatsoever ye shall loose on earth shall be loosed in heaven.

Notice that the word "earth" comes before the word "heaven" in each one of the statements. Notice that the binding and loosening starts in *earth*. It does not start in heaven and come down to earth. That tells me that it is my choice, that I have something to do with it, and that thrills me. In the following chapters of this book, we will look at these four biblical facts in detail.

8

#1 — What We Are In Christ

We must confess WHAT WE ARE IN CHRIST if we expect to live the victorious Christian life. This statement refers to your standing with God. In other words, how do you stand with God? According to God's Word, the Bible, you are everything God says you are, whether you are presently experiencing it or not. You are because God says so. If you are not living up to that level, that is your problem, not God's.

If you are not what God says you are, then God lied. And if God lied about that, how do you know what part of His Word is the truth and what part is a lie? You do not. Either it is all a lie or it is all the truth.

When I was saved and began attending church, I was not told how I stood with God. The only thing I was told was that I was just a sinner saved by grace. So how could I confess what I did not know?

I want to go through the scriptures and point you to a few choice statements, the kind that I would encourage you to search out for yourself. This will be a starter course, so to speak, an appetizer, so that you can get an idea of what you should be confessing. We *must* confess God's Word if we are to overcome the onslaught of defeatism that the enemy has brought, and will continue to bring against us to prevent us from living a victorious Christian life.

God wants you to be a winner. Whether you realize it or not, God only operates with *winning*. There is *no defeat* in God, even though for years we have been sold a bill of goods by those who supposedly represent Him. They told us, "Sometimes up and sometimes down, and sometimes almost level to the ground." But that is not in the Bible. We are everything that the Word of God says we are.

In 2 Corinthians 5:17, we have a very familiar verse, but a verse so important to us as Christians.

> **Therefore if any man be in Christ, he is a new creature: old things are passed away; behold, all things are become new.**

We understand when He talks about "man," he is using the word generically, and it means male or female; but it means man as opposed to animals.

If *any man* be in Christ.... How does a person get in Christ? By being born again! In other words, by doing what Romans 10:9 says,

> **That if thou shalt confess with thy mouth the Lord Jesus, and shalt believe in thine heart that God hath raised him from the dead, thou shalt be saved.**

If you have done that, then you are in Christ and Christ is in you.

...**he is a new creature....** Actually, the word, "creature," is misleading. It should be, literally, "creation." You were originally a creation of God, but now you are a new creation. What does "new" tell you? It refers to something that has never been before. That is what God says you are — something that you have never been before.

Let me, however, qualify a few things in this verse. It says ...**old things are passed away....** If old things have passed away, that means the old things no longer exist. Is that a fair estimate? It further states, **Behold, all things are become new.** We have to define what are the *old things* that passed away and what are the *all things* that have become new. In that way, we can pinpoint where we are old and where we are new, so that we will know how to relate to what God says about us.

Only Your Spirit is New

Right away, if you are not careful, you will naturally assume that this is talking about being a brand new person all over. If I am a brand new person all over, then that means I am brand new physically. In most churches, we have not been told that we are more than flesh and blood. We have heard the word "soul," but we did not know what it meant. The words "body" and "soul" were about all we were familiar with.

We would assume that if we are a new creation, then we are new in our bodies, but we are not. There is nothing new about your body — it is the same body you had before being saved. I submit to you that the physical part of you did not pass away, and that all things did not become new in your body. And that is easy to prove.

If old things passed away in your physical body, it would mean that if you had false teeth before, you should have a brand new set of natural teeth in your mouth now, and you know that is not true. If you were baldheaded the day before you got saved, you still have no hair on your cranial cavity the day after! The point I am making, and I am not trying to be funny, is that physically, we are the same.

When a woman gives birth to a baby, physically her body goes through a traumatic change. Likewise, there is something that happens to you spiritually when you are born again. You feel highly exhilarated when you are born again. When you come in contact with God and Christ, it is a joyous, almost unexplainable experience. It affects your whole being and it is awesome.

The woman who gives birth to the baby goes through a trauma experience, but it does come to an end. When the baby is birthed, it is over, and then she returns to what is called normalcy. In like manner, when you are born again, you go through a birth experience, but it comes to an end and you settle back into a normalcy; only this time, it ought to be a normalcy in the framework of the Word of God.

That is the area where many people miss it. Because when you first come in contact with Christ, it is so exhilarating, so thrilling, so wonderful, you think you are going to stay like that the rest of your life. However, that exhilarating state was never designed to last any more than it was designed for the woman, once she gives birth to the baby, to stay in that same *state of giving birth* to the baby for the next 20 years without giving birth to the baby. That only comes with giving birth to the baby.

When you go through the new birth, your spirit becomes brand new. God puts a brand new spirit in you. After you experience the trauma of the new birth, you settle back down into a normal mode of living, except this normalcy ought to be spiritually motivated based on God's Word. But if you do not know that, you will return to living like you were before you ever came in contact with Jesus. Your physical body will end up governing you and directing you. Your old mind that has not yet been renewed by the Word of God will gravitate back to doing the same things you used to do, thinking the same things you used to think. The only difference is, you will start feeling a twinge of conscience when you do those things. You know that something is wrong, and you should not have done it, but you did it, and somehow you feel like you cannot help yourself. When you were made new, only your spirit was made brand new. What are the old things that passed away?

In your spirit, before you become a Christian, you are alienated and separated from God. You are in a state of what is called "spiritual death," a state of "sin consciousness." After you receive Jesus, you are no longer alienated and separated from God. You no longer have spiritual death abiding in you. You are now a new creature in Christ Jesus.

You now have the life of God in you. I am alive to God, and my past, spiritually speaking, is over.

Since I am a new creature, I have to guard my mouth so that I do not say what Satan attempts to infiltrate into my unrenewed mind about who I used to be, to get me to return to that former level of existence. Satan wants to get me back to that former kind of thinking, that kind of action, and most importantly, that kind of confession.

Your old mind that has not yet been renewed by the Word of God will gravitate back to doing the same things you used to do, thinking the same things you used to think. The only difference is, you will start feeling a twinge of conscience when you do those things. You know that something is wrong, and you should not have done it, but you did it, and somehow you feel like you cannot help yourself.

God said I am a new creature. I need to stand in front of the mirror of my life and say, "Praise God, I am a brand new creature. I am not what I used to be; therefore, I must seek new avenues of adventure. I must seek new levels of operation, because I am no longer the person that I used to be. I cannot see myself that way anymore." I may have to change where I go and with whom I associate. I may have to change my so-called friends. This goes for any born-again believer. You may have to make a new list of friends and a new list of places to go. Because there is a new person on the inside, you cannot operate on the same level as before.

God's design is that my spirit man, that man on the inside, feed on the Word of God so that the Word of God, through my spirit, will direct and change my mind or soul, so that my mind can tell my body what to do in line with God's Word.

The devil has very cleverly kept most Christians from personally reading the Bible. He does not mind you going to church. He does not mind you whooping and hollering. He does not mind you singing loud and making a lot of noise, because there is no life in that.

You have churches full of people who love the Lord, and have had genuine experience with God, but their bodies control, dominate, and direct their lives. My body controlled me, too, until I found out how to control it. I thought all those cravings I had were normal. I said, "I am just doing what comes naturally." Naturally sinning, naturally messing up, naturally doing what was wrong.

I did not understand. I thought my body was new, until I found out differently. I now keep my body under lock and key. I do not trust my body. I never let it out of my sight. Your body is not what is saved. We have to understand that. Your standing with God is a spiritual standing, not a physical one. We, as Christians, live our lives in a physical context, but it should be spiritually motivated.

Now, **If any man be in Christ, he is a new creature: old things are passed away; behold, all things are become new.** That is who God says I am. I am a new creature. I cannot lie anymore. I cannot steal anymore, because God said I am new. When the devil comes with his temptation, I say, "No, I can't do that, devil, because I am new." If you still think you are the same old wretch that you used to be, what do you expect a wretch to do but mess up? So, it is very easy to gravitate back to sin. Like the Bible says about the dog, he returns to his vomit. He does not know any better. But you know better, because you are a new creature in Christ Jesus.

You are everything that God says you are. That is what the statement "we walk by faith and not by sight" means. I use that scripture all the time. When you walk by faith, it simply means you walk by what God says in His Word. And that seems so hard for people to grasp and understand. They still let their emotions (their soul), and their bodies (their flesh), get involved. God's Word is what should direct my life, and it is by faith I do it.

I have to ignore signals from my body and thoughts from my mind. I have to operate strictly by what the Word says. If I do not, I will be messed up and so will you. You will be up one day and down the next. You will be on the "yo-yo syndrome." You certainly do not want to be that way. You should want to be constant, but you will never be constant unless you operate by faith.

That is why I harp on faith all the time. Twenty years ago the Lord impressed upon me that faith is the key to everything. In essence, the Lord said, "Fred, if you ever get that into your spirit where it becomes the watch-word of your life, you will be able to master and overcome any and everything that ever attempts to come against you. You can NEVER BE DEFEATED, if you learn to walk by faith."

If you walk by signs, if you walk by your body, it is constantly in flux, constantly changing. There are all kinds of things Satan will throw against you to affect your body. He will trick you into thinking that if a thought comes into your mind, that means you thought it up and so it is just as bad to *think* it, as it is to do it. And since you thought it, you might as well go ahead and do it. That is a lie right out of the pit of hell! Do not fall for that garbage.

I do not care what kind of thoughts come in your mind, do not get into a guilt trip when those thoughts come. I am not telling you to sit around all day thinking about pornography. Negative thoughts come to everyone, but the issue is, what do you do with them? Evidence abounds as to what some people do with them. Yes! They yield to them and go ahead and do what the thought said. You have to resist that negative thought. And you can do it, because you are new, and none of that old behavior is in the new, spiritual creation.

If you were walking down the street and saw a pile of cow manure, you would not have any problem resisting the temptation to go pick it up and have it for lunch! You may say, "That is gross!" But so is fornication, oral sex, homosexuality, lesbianism, alcoholism, and drugs. And if you develop that kind of attitude — that it is gross, that it is cow manure — you will keep your hands off of it! In fact, to get right down to the nitty gritty, it would do you better to eat some of that cow manure than to suck on that cancer stick (cigarette) or sniff and smoke that cocaine.

That is the kind of attitude you ought to have about all those things out there. Treat them like the Bible says, like dung, which means manure. And I do not have a problem resisting manure, do you? You have to use whatever you have at hand, to keep you out of trouble.

Would you pull the sheets back on a bed and lie down on a mattress of cow manure? Well, when you are tempted to get in bed with someone who is not your spouse, see that bed as cow manure and you will put your clothes on and get out of that place!

I would wager there are some reading this book right now, who wish they had thought about that years ago, right? Some are paying right now for things they did twenty-five years ago. They wish to God they had thought of it as cow manure then, and they would not be in the mess they are now.

We Are Complete In Him

Colossians 2:9,10:

> **For in him dwelleth all the fullness of the Godhead bodily. And ye are complete in him, which is the head of all principality and power.**

You are what? What does complete mean? It means entire. Okay, if you are complete, if you are entire, if you are whole, then you are lacking nothing. How can I be complete in Him, and have an inferiority complex? If I am complete in Him, how can I have low self-esteem? We have been listening to the devil's lie, telling us what we are not, instead of listening to God's Word, which tells us that we are complete.

And what will happen is that when you begin to see yourself as complete and begin to confess that, speaking life to your life, it will cause you to live up to what you say about you. It is not a psych job. It is releasing the power of God, and that is the way the power of God is released, by the words that we speak. It is not psyching yourself out, because you do not have to psych yourself out.

We just read it. The Book said, "We are complete in Christ." If we are not complete in Christ, then God lied to us and the Bible says He cannot lie, so we must be complete.

We need to see ourselves as God sees us. We are complete in Christ, which is the head of all principality and power. We are in Christ, so we are complete. When people do not understand that, they will think you are arrogant. They will think you are a braggart, braggadocios, self-centered. But you cannot be intimidated by that. You have to know who you are, because God said so.

You are whole in Christ. Do you realize that? There is nothing left out of you. When God gave you that new re-created human spirit, there was no shortage in it. You have to see yourself as a new creation, and then you will begin to think and talk about yourself that way, and all of a sudden, you will find yourself *acting* as a new person who demonstrates the righteousness of Christ. You will begin to act in character with the way Jesus would act.

A dog barks because he is a dog. That is the language of a dog. You do not hear dogs going "moo." It is not their nature. It is natural for a dog to bark, for a cat to meow, and for a cow to moo, because that is their nature. Well, you have the nature of God, and in that nature of God, there is completeness.

I am a whole person in God. Now, that does not mean that I do not have to work on sharpening myself up, but I have all of the necessary ingredients. There is nothing that is left out, and if I will keep mixing the "cake-mix" with my tongue, in terms of confessing who I am, I will finally get the batter — my life — just the way it is supposed to be. And I will have a beautiful cake with icing and candles on top!

I have to see myself that way and say that about myself, and not let anybody tell me who I am or what I am. I am what God says I am, and I say what God says, so I am what I say I am. It does not matter to me what you think. It does not move me in the least. Think whatever you want.

I do not care what my wife thinks about me. I know my wife loves me, because she told me, and her word is good just like God's Word is good. I believe that, but what I am saying is it would not matter what she thought about me. I am not what I am because my wife thinks that is who I am. I am that because God says I am that.

Colossians 1:12,13:

> Giving thanks unto the Father, which hath made us meet (which means *able)* to be partakers of the inheritance of the saints in light:
>
> Who hath delivered us from the power of darkness, and hath translated us into the kingdom of his dear Son.

In verse 13, the old English word, "hath," means the same thing as has. In this context, it has a past tense designation. It indicates that the time of action has already taken place. It is not in the process of taking place, or shall or will take place in the future, it is already done. That is exciting to me ...**who has delivered us....** Make it personal ...**who hath delivered me....** That means every one of us. He told me He has delivered me. From what? That word, "power," means the authority or dominion of darkness.

The word "darkness" in this scripture does not mean night time. It is talking about the kingdom of Satan. It tells us in the same verse that we have been translated into the kingdom of His dear Son. You are in somebody's kingdom all the time. Either in the kingdom of darkness or the kingdom of light. You are in the kingdom of God or in the kingdom of Satan.

And since He has delivered me from the kingdom or the authority or the power of the dominion of darkness, I do not need any deliverance. I am delivered! God said I am and God cannot lie. When I say I do not need to be delivered, I am not making an arrogant statement. I am making a statement of fact based upon the Word of God.

How do I speak life to my life with that fact? I begin to say, "Praise God, I am free. Praise God I am delivered from anything that would hold me in bondage; *anything,* whether it is sex, women, men, cigarettes, whiskey, gambling, lying, fear, whatever. I have been delivered from it."

You might not actually be experiencing that deliverance at a specific point in time, but that is not because you are not delivered. It is only because you do not know any better and you are continuing to accept the bondage. You continue to confess, "Well, I have a problem with sex."

The Word says we can speak death or life to our life. You do not have enough Bible sense to realize it yet, and that is why you are having the problem. It is because you are confessing it. And you do not hear what you are saying. YOU ARE TYING THE ROPE AROUND YOUR OWN LIFE BY SAYING, "I have a problem with sex. I have a problem with cigarettes. I have a problem with homosexuality. I have a problem with narcotics. I have . . . ." *That* is why you *have* it, because YOU SAID YOU DO! God said He set you free from it, you said you have it.

If you can ever get this into your spirit where it affects your thinking, when you get ready to pick up that cigarette, you will say, "Wait a minute! What am I doing?! I am free! I have been delivered. I do not need this devilish thing. Get away from me in the name of Jesus!" But if you continue saying you are in bondage, what do you expect a person in bondage to do? Go right back and wallow in the mud!

Say, "I am free! That is below my dignity. I have been set free. I cannot indulge in this kind of activity. I am free. I used to be in bondage to cocaine. I used to be hung up on sex. I used to be this, that, or the other, but I am free. He set me free!" I have to speak that to my life. I have to tell me that every day. I have to say it until I am actually experiencing it and that is what releases the power.

When you walk into a room and flip the switch on the wall, that is not what creates light, that simply releases the electricity to the light bulb for your benefit. The light is actually potentially there all the time, as long as you pay your electric bill. But you have to flip the switch or push a button to activate it. It is there all the time in essence, but not in manifestation. When you flip the switch, you activate it. It becomes manifest at that point. Do you understand?

Well, likewise, God's deliverance is in you, if you are a child of God. It is already there, but you have to activate it. How do you flip the switch? With your mouth, by saying, "I am free. I have been delivered. I have been set free. I am no longer in bondage!" And then you start acting like that.

How to Act Like You Are Delivered

How does a person who is not in bondage act? How does a person act who is free from nicotine? You do not buy any more cigarettes! You do not have any reason to go to the cigarette machine, because you are free from cigarettes. You no longer have to meet the pusher on the corner because you are not under the influence of narcotics. What do you need a pusher for? YOU ARE FREE! You do not need to go to the liquor store. You do not drink anymore, you are delivered from alcoholism. A non-drinker has no need to go to the place where they are dispensing alcoholic beverages, right?

If you come to my house, one thing is conspicuous in its absence — you will not find an ash tray in my house. What does a non-smoker need with an ash tray? Are you following me? So, if you have been delivered from nicotine and cigarettes, you have no need for an ash tray. What do you need a cigarette lighter for?

Because you are not married and you are delivered from sexual things, then you keep your chastity belt locked, because unmarried people in Christ do not need sex, right?! You are free.

Some people in their squeamish, petrified, fearful perception of God will say, "Brother Price, you can't make any demands on God. You don't have any rights with God!" Who says so? No, I cannot *arbitrarily* DEMAND rights, but I am not doing that. All I am doing is demanding the rights that God said I already have, and *I am not demanding them from God,* because it is not God Who is attempting to keep them from me. I am demanding them from the evil one who I have been delivered from.

The evil one does not like the fact that I am delivered and he wants to keep me in bondage. He wants to put dark shades over my eyes so that I will not know the truth, and keep me under his foot. But I KNOW THAT I HAVE BEEN SET FREE! "LOOSE ME, DEVIL, AND LET ME GO!"

God said it. I believe it, and that forever settles it. I have deliverance. So, I started acting like I had it. I started acting like a free person would act, and I started talking like a free person would talk. FREE AT LAST, FREE AT LAST, THANK GOD ALMIGHTY, I AM FREE AT LAST!

From The Curse To The Blessing

Galatians 3:13 says, Christ hath redeemed us from the curse. If you are from somewhere, that means that you are *not presently* where you are *from*. Because if you were presently where you are from, you would be there, you would not be *from* there. I could rightfully, biblically, scripturally say, "I am *from* the curse." That is telling you I am not in the curse now, which means that I am no longer where the curse is. I am somewhere else. And I could easily see that the opposite of the curse would be the blessing.

Let us prove that from the Word so that we do not get into speculation.

Galatians 3:13,14:

Christ hath redeemed us from the curse of the law, being made a curse for us: for it is written, Cursed is every one that hangeth on a tree:

That the blessing of Abraham might come on the Gentiles through Jesus Christ; that we might receive the promise of the Spirit through faith.

Christ has redeemed us from the curse so that the blessing can come. You see, the blessing and the curse cannot occupy the same point in time. You either have the curse or you have the blessing. You cannot have both. You either have dark or you have light. You cannot have both. Dark is the absence of light, and light is the absence of dark. You cannot have light and dark at the same point in time.

Christ has redeemed us from the curse. That is who I am. I am from the curse. You thought my name was Fred Price, but my name is really, "From the Curse." Can you see that? That is where I am from. If I am from the curse, then I am somewhere else. Where am I? I am in the blessing.

What is the curse? I need to know what I have been redeemed *from* so that I can know what I have been redeemed *to*.

Deuteronomy 28:15:

> But it shall come to pass, if thou wilt not hearken (which means to "listen") unto the voice of the Lord thy God, to observe to do all his commandments and his statutes which I command thee this day; that all these curses shall come upon thee, and overtake thee.

Observe to do WHAT? Wait a minute! How can they come upon thee and overtake thee if they are not already in existence? An automobile on the highway cannot overtake me unless that automobile is on the same highway that I am on. The implication is that these curses are already on the same highway that man is on. However, whenever I observe to do all that is written in God's Word, I will stay ahead of the curses.

Notice also in that verse, the word, "commandment." What is the first thing you think of when you hear that word? Ten commandments. We are so traditionally oriented to this ten commandment business, that when we hear the word, "commandments," right away, we think of ten commandments.

I submit to you that this word, "commandments" is a synonym for God's Word, which is God's will. And I have news for you, it is *not* limited to *ten*! It means anything and everything that God tells you to do. The reason that it is called "commandment" is because whenever God Almighty speaks to you, it is *not a suggestion*.

Deuteronomy 28:16-19:

> Cursed shalt thou be in the city, and cursed shalt thou be in the field.
>
> Cursed shall be thy basket and thy store.

Cursed shall be the fruit of thy body, and the fruit of thy land, the increase of thy kine, and the flocks of thy sheep.

Cursed shalt thou be when thou comest in, and cursed shalt thou be when thou goest out.

In verse 20 of that chapter it begins to say, **The Lord shall send upon thee....** But this is one of those statements that should read, "The Lord will *permit* to be sent...."

Verse 15 tells of all the curses that shall come and overtake thee. That implies they are already there. But take this example as an illustration: The Travelers Insurance Company's logo is a red umbrella. Around the umbrella, rain is falling. Underneath the umbrella, it is dry. The point is that if you are covered by that insurance company, you are protected from all of those adverse things. The rain is representative of automobile accidents, fires, hazards, etc.

The Word of God is like that umbrella. As long as you stay under it, observe to do all that God says, then you have the umbrella. The umbrella — God's Word — does not stop the curses from coming, nor does it do away with the curses so that they are no longer existent. But what it does is keep the rain from falling on you.

If you keep up the umbrella of God's protection, you can walk right through the storm, and walk out dry! But if you do not *observe to do,* the curses, which are already there, will come upon you. That means you do not have an umbrella now. You have no protection. The way it is worded in verse 19 makes it appear God is doing the *cursing.* It should have been rendered, "The Lord will permit to be brought."

Now I want to show you something else. This should help some of you who have been sitting around all your Christian life nursing some ailment like arthritis, bursitis, heart condition, varicose veins, or whatever it might be. You have been nursing the thing, thinking you were suffering for the Lord, not realizing you are suffering because you are ignorant of God's Word.

Deuteronomy 28:61:

> **Also every sickness, and every plague, which is not written in the book of this law, them will the Lord** (permit to be brought) **bring upon thee, until thou be destroyed.**

Verses 20-28 talk about all kinds of diseases that affect every part of your body. But then he goes on to say, God will permit to come upon you even the things that are not written in the Book.

What am I saying? I am saying, for you who have been nursing your condition, thinking you were serving God, thinking God *wanted* you to hold on and keep a stiff upper lip, and never give up and always praise Him right in the middle of all that sickness and disease — you ought to be able to tell by this that the sickness and disease were *not* from God. It is *not* the will of God!

God does not want you to have it, because it is a curse of the law. You have been nursing a curse. That arthritis is not a blessing from God. IT IS A CURSE! And you do not have any business with it! You do not have to have it. You can repudiate it. You can renounce it and get rid of it. God does not want you to have it, but you will, as long as you disobey His Word.

The thing that is so awesome and tragic about this is that even if you do not know what His will is, you are going to pay the consequences anyway. That is why He gave you a Book you can read for yourself. You do not have to depend on Fred Price or any other minister of the Gospel. They ought to be telling you the truth, and I am, but that does not make any difference.

The bottom line is God is going to hold you accountable — especially you who live in America — you have no excuse. You can buy a Bible at the drug store. You can go to a hotel and spend one night in a room and find a Bible in the drawer. You have no excuse in America not to know the will of God. If you really want to know it, you can know it, and God is going to hold you accountable for it.

Sickness and disease are curses. They are not blessings. God wants you to avoid it, and He tells you exactly how to do it. *Observe to do!*

If you observe to do, to follow His statutes, then these things cannot come upon you and overtake you. So that means it is not God's will for me to have them. You have been redeemed. But if you do not know that, you cannot take advantage of it.

It is sad to say it, but the organized church world has been playing games, entertaining folk. It is pathetic and I really feel sorry for the ministers. They will have to stand before Jesus Christ and give an account for what they have done with God's people.

It is tragic, but I did not learn anything about these truths in churches that I went to over a seventeen-year period. They did not tell me anything about this. They did not tell me that there was a curse. They did not tell me that if I observed to do the Word of God that I could be exonerated from that curse. They did not tell me about the blessing of Abraham. They did not tell me that Christ has redeemed me from the curse of the law.

Jesus told us that if the blind lead the blind, they both end up in the microwave oven, burnt beyond recognition. God said it many years ago through the mouth of the prophet, **My people are destroyed** (or "perish") **for lack of knowledge** (Hos. 4:6). Perish, how? With this curse. Because the curse is blind. It comes on everyone. It has no preference. One thing about the curse, it is definitely not prejudiced. Christ has redeemed us from the curse.

The Blessing of Abraham

We are still discussing WHAT WE ARE IN CHRIST. What am I? I am the redeemed. I have a standing with God. I am His purchased, blood-bought, blood-washed son. I am a son of God. I am the redeemed of the Lord and I am saying so. Christ has redeemed me *from* the curse of the law so that the *BLESSING* of *ABRAHAM* might come upon me.

Here is what is so exciting about it, that God has forever settled this issue in heaven. God has made it so abundantly clear that you would have to *hire* someone and pay them overtime to help you misunderstand this.

We read what the curse is and we are going to read a description of the blessing. But before we do, I want to make sure you know that the scriptures we read are talking about YOU. Sometimes people hear things and they think they cannot relate to it. They cannot believe that this could mean them. So, you need to know that God is talking about YOU.

Galatians 3:14:

That the blessing of Abraham might come on the Gentiles through Jesus Christ; that we might receive the promise of the Spirit through faith.

Abraham lived before the Old Testament or covenant was instituted. However, the story about Abraham is contained in the context of the Old Covenant.

Galatians 3:7:

Know ye therefore that they which are of faith, the same are the children of Abraham.

Abraham is called the father of the faithful. What does that mean? This is letting us know we have a spiritual relationship to Abraham, in that Abraham was a man of faith. He believed God, the Bible said. Jesus Christ did not come to the earth during the time that Abraham lived. He did not die at Calvary during the time Abraham lived. Jesus did not rise from the dead during the time Abraham lived.

And since Jesus Christ did not ascend to the right hand of the Father after having risen from the grave during the time Abraham lived, Abraham could never accept Jesus Christ as his personal Savior and Lord. He never had that opportunity.

If Abraham could not accept Jesus Christ as his personal Savior and Lord, that would mean that Abraham could never be WHAT? BORN AGAIN! If Abraham could never be born again, that would mean that Abraham could never be WHAT? Saved! In other words, he could never become a Christian.

As a result of all of this, that means that Abraham could not participate in anything spiritual, because he would be dead in trespasses and sin. In other words, he would be spiritually dead.

If God blessed Abraham before Jesus came to this world, it means that there is only one thing that God could have blessed Abraham with, and that would have to be material things, because he was not spiritually alive. He could not relate to God spiritually because Christ had not come.

The Bible says in Acts 4:12:

Neither is there salvation in any other: for there is none other name under heaven given among men, whereby we must be saved.

That name was not given to Abraham, so how could he be saved? He could not. If he was not saved, then he was a sinner. Just like anybody who lives today who has not yet accepted Christ is a sinner. Abraham was a sinner and God had to deal with Abraham as a sinner, as a physical man, not as a spiritual man.

When the Bible says that ''the blessing of Abraham might come on the Gentiles,'' then that blessing must be a physical blessing. We get our spiritual blessing from where? JESUS! Because Jesus has come, Jesus has died,

Jesus HAS RISEN, Jesus has ascended and we can and have accepted Him, therefore, our spiritual relationship with God comes as a result of our connection with Jesus. But our physical relationship with God comes as the result of our connection with Abraham, our faithful father.

Also consider Galatians 3:9:

So then they which be of faith are blessed with faithful Abraham.

When it says we who are of faith are the children of Abraham, it means that like Abraham believed God and God gave him credit for being righteous, as we believe God by faith, we are declared righteous. So, in that sense, they that are of faith are the children of Abraham.

When you find out how Abraham was blessed, you will understand why the material aspect of the Gospel is so often criticized. The purpose of the criticism is to frighten you off and intimidate you from ever moving into it. Satan knows that if you ever become financially and materially independent of the circumstances, you will then have at your fingertips, the resources to promote the Gospel like it ought to be promoted, without any hindrances. And he knows if that happens, there will be an onslaught made against the gates of his kingdom, and those gates will not be able to stand against the onslaught of the Word of God. Because you see, it costs big money to promote the Gospel.

The curse and blessing are revealed in Deuteronomy 28:1-3:

And it shall come to pass, (that is God speaking through the mouth of the prophet) **if thou shalt hearken diligently unto the voice of the LORD thy God, to observe AND to do all his commandments which I command thee this day, that the Lord thy God will set thee on high above all nations of the earth:**

And all these blessings shall come on thee, AND overtake thee. . . .

Blessed shalt thou be in the city, and blessed shalt thou be in the field.

You do not have to move to the suburbs to be blessed. People have been migrating from the inner cities of our nation to the seclusion and, in their mind, the safety of the suburbs. Some people believe God can only operate outside the city limits. They believe God is handicapped if you stay in the inner city and that He can only work in the suburbs.

He said, **Blessed shalt thou be in the city....** I am not leaving the city myself. You can spend 65-90 minutes going one way trying to get away from the city and drive to the suburb and beat your brains out on the freeways every day if you want to, smelling all that exhaust smoke for 90 minutes or more.

Some of you were born in the suburbs. To you, that was life. So, you do not have to leave the suburbs, the fields, to come into the city to be blessed. You can be blessed where you are, if you hearken unto the voice of the Lord your God. So you can be blessed in the suburbs, and I can be blessed in the city, close to my home and my job. I do not have to get on a freeway to get to my home or to my job! Amen! Hallelujah. Eat your heart out, you daily freeway drivers!

Deuteronomy 28:4

Blessed shall be the fruit of thy body... (That is talking about childbearing. Your seed will be blessed. That is good news. You can expect to have a healthy baby, if you know how to use your faith.) **and the fruit of thy ground** (notice that He said the fruit of YOUR ground), **and the fruit of thy cattle, the increase of thy kine** (that is a special kind of cattle), **and the flocks of thy sheep.**

God is saying *anything* you are involved with ought to be blessed. My ground is my ministry. The ministry that God entrusted to me. This is soil, the ground that I have to work and plant in. I do not care what somebody else's ground is doing. I do not have to listen to those who might say, "This is all you can do here in this part of the city, because this is a blighted area, this is the ghetto." Yes, but did you know that both garden and ghetto begin with a "G." So you can turn the ghetto into a garden, a garden of Eden if you have the faith to believe it.

It is up to you whether your ground is blessed or not. I am expecting a harvest, and I am expecting a BIG HARVEST. A GIGANTIC, BRONTOSAURUS-SIZED HARVEST! Because I am planting good seed in that ground, and my Father God told me, "Blessed shall be the fruit of thy ground." This is my ground, so I expect my ministry to work. I expect my ministry to grow. I expect my ministry to produce results in the lives of others, because that is the seed I am planting, the Word of God, and your lives are the soil in which that seed is planted.

I am expecting results. I am supposed to have everything I want to have and everything I can believe God for. I have it recorded in my Father's Word.

There is a spiritual law of sowing and reaping — thank God that no man can abrogate it. If you plant good seed into good ground, you will get a harvest, and nobody can stop it. The classroom may be your ground. Or the filling station may be your ground. But wherever you are, that is your ground and you ought to expect for it to be blessed. If you are doing all of the things that the voice of the Lord has called upon you to do and everything you know how to do.

Deuteronomy 28:5:

Blessed shall be thy basket and thy store.

The basket and store represented what was brought and stored up until it was needed, because they did not use everything right away. When I was a little boy, my parents used to store preserves. Throughout the winter, we would eat good vegetables and fruits from those jars of preserves, or canned goods.

In this day and age, perhaps your basket and store is your bank account, or your investments. If you are spending everything you get and have nothing left over, then you are not blessed yet. Your basket and store should be blessed.

Deuteronomy 28:6

Blessed shalt thou be when thou comest in, and blessed shalt thou be when thou goest out.

In other words, a blessing should be waiting for when you leave home and go out into the street. Are you getting the message that God wants you blessed? I love it! Many of you are missing out on it because you are not looking for the blessing. Do you look for it? We often pass right over things that are blessings, because we are looking for some great big atomic explosion. God does not always speak in the thunder. Sometimes it is the still small voice. You have to be sensitive and open so that you do not miss out on your blessings.

Sometimes things can seem so inconsequential that you miss it and take it for granted, yet it could be the blessing of your life. I expect to be blessed when I go out and blessed when I come in. God told me I am BLESSED, *not* cursed.

Deuteronomy 28:7,8:

The Lord shall cause thine enemies that rise up against thee to be smitten before thy face: they shall come out against thee one way, and flee before thee seven ways. (Wow! If that is not protection, I do not know what is.)

The Lord shall command the blessing upon thee in thy storehouses, and in all that thou settest thine hand unto; and he shall bless thee in the land which the Lord thy God giveth thee.

At the time this was enunciated, it was spoken from a historical point of view, to Israel, so some of it would have immediate application to the Israelites as they were about to go into the land that God had promised them. But ultimately, the truth was for all generations of the people of God.

God has given us a land. We have been translated out of darkness into the kingdom of God's dear Son. That land is the land of walking in the realm of the Spirit. Our land flows with milk and honey, so to speak, and we are supposed to be blessed and victorious in that land. We are supposed to enjoy it.

He said my *storehouses* shall be blessed. My storehouse would be wherever I am storing up something. Like your bank account, your investment portfolio. That means I should make the highest rate of interest available, compounded daily. I ought to be blessed so that I can be a blessing. Everything you set your hand to, God will command the blessing upon it. That is why I believe my ministry is blessed and always will be blessed.

Psalm 1:1-3:

Blessed is the man that walketh not in the counsel of the ungodly, nor standeth in the way of sinners, nor sitteth in the seat of the scornful.

But his delight is in the law of the Lord; and in his law doth he meditate day and night.

And he shall be like a tree planted by the rivers of water, that bringeth forth his fruit in his season; his leaf also shall not wither; and whatsoever he doeth shall *prosper*.

That sounds exactly like . . . **blessed in all that you set your hand to.** He said whatsoever you do, it shall prosper. So, I confess that. "I am blessed going out and I am blessed coming in. I am blessed in all that I do." When I say that, I am speaking life to my life and that creates the reality of it in my life.

Deuteronomy 28:9-11:

The Lord shall establish thee an holy people unto himself, as he hath sworn unto thee, if thou shalt keep the commandments of the Lord thy God, and walk in his ways.

And all people of the earth shall see that thou art called by the name of the Lord; and they shall be afraid of thee.

And the Lord shall make thee plenteous in goods, in the fruit of thy body (your body should produce fruitfully, you should not be barren), **and in the fruit of thy cattle, and in the fruit of thy ground, in the land which the Lord sware unto thy fathers to give thee.**

The people of Israel spent their labor in the field, with the cattle, living off the land. They were an agrarian society. Whatever your area of endeavor is where you spend your labor. He said you will have plenty of goods — predicated, of course, on your hearkening unto the voice of the Lord your God and observing to do. If you are not listening, seeing, and doing, then these things will not be manifested in your life.

Remember, the land that the Lord has given us is the kingdom of God when we were born again. We still live in the world, we are physical creatures, but we are not limited to and should not be governed by the world system.

Deuteronomy 28:12:

The Lord shall open unto thee his good treasure, the heaven to give the rain unto thy land in his season (whenever rain destroys, that is *not* God), **and to bless all the work of thine hand: and thou shalt lend unto many nations, and thou shalt not borrow.**

How can the Lord open unto you His good treasure? Simple, because He has no bad treasure. God is good, so His treasure would have to be good. Jesus made reference to such when He said, *You cannot get sweet water out of a bitter fountain. You do not get grapes off of a bramble bush. Everything produces after its kind.*

James 1:17 is a New Testament scripture that corroborates what I have said:

Every good gift and every perfect gift is from above, and cometh down from the Father of lights, with whom is no variableness, neither shadow of turning.

If every good gift and every perfect gift is from above, then every bad gift and every imperfect gift is from beneath or below. So, whatever is hellish in nature comes from hell. And whatever is heavenly in nature comes from heaven. And because there is no variableness, He does not ever change. He is consistent. He cannot be good one day and bad the next. If His good ever becomes bad, then it is variable, it has changed and that would invalidate His Word. That ought to be good news for you!

Let me ask you a very pointed question: Have *you* hearkened unto the voice of the Lord? Have *you* observed? Are *you* doing? If your answer is "Yes!" then say these words: "ALL THE WORK OF MY HAND IS PROSPERING, WILL PROSPER, CAN DO NOTHING ELSE BUT PROSPER, BECAUSE I HAVE HEARKENED UNTO THE VOICE OF THE LORD AND I HAVE OBSERVED TO DO ALL OF HIS COMMANDMENTS (WORDS)."

Deuteronomy 28:12 tells us that **we shall lend unto many nations and shalt not borrow. And the Lord shall make thee plenteous in goods.** You will be able to lend and not have to borrow because you will have plenty!

There are many people in the charismatic renewal and in this so called "faith walk" who believe that you should not borrow anything from a lending institution, and they cite Deuteronomy 28:12 as a proof text. But this verse does not say it is *wrong* to borrow. It simply says you will have so much, you will not *have* to do the borrowing, because you will be the one doing the lending.

It is obvious that borrowing could not be wrong, because if so, then lending would have to be wrong, since it is the lending that causes borrowing.

I think that the Body of Christ should be the nation that does the lending — not necessarily to the nations of the world, but to the nations of the Body of Christ. You could think of a state as a nation or you could think of a group of people as a nation, or you could think of a local church or congregation as a nation that may need money. We could lend to them, but we *cannot* if we do not have it.

Deuteronomy 28:13:

> **And the Lord shall make thee the head, and not the tail; and thou shalt be above only, and thou shalt not be beneath; if that thou hearken unto the commandments of the Lord thy God, which command thee this day, to observe and to do them:**

Do you like that? The *head* and not the *tail,* because when you are the tail, you get wagged by somebody else. Tails do not wag dogs, dogs wag tails. If we are the tail, we get wagged, and, in this case, by Satan.

What are we in Christ? We are the blessed. We are the plenteous in goods. We are the head; we are not the tail. We are above and not beneath. You need to *confess* that. You need to see yourself that way. No matter what circumstances may present to your view, you must look at the circumstances and point the finger of the Word of God at them and tell them, "I am the blessed of the Lord. I am not the cursed!"

At first you may not see any change in those circumstances when you begin to say that, but you must be consistent. It is like a farmer. You cannot plant a seed on Monday and expect a harvest on Tuesday. Then because you don't see the results on Tuesday, you dig up the field. You will never get a harvest that way. The farmer has to believe the seed is working, that the seed he planted is alive. So what does he do? He waters it on a daily basis. He sees weeds coming up, so he plucks the weeds up so they do not choke the seed.

The farmer has not seen a thing, yet it is amazing the faith that he has in the seed. He is watering it. That is what we have to do with our words. We plant the seed of God's Word in our lives by our words, and then we water it continually with the words of our mouth: "Praise God, I believe I am healed. Thank You, Father, I believe I am healed." What am I doing? I am watering.

When I first said it, I said, "With His stripes I was healed," I *planted*. Then every day after that, until I see the harvest, the manifestation in my physical body, I water: "Father, thank You, I believe I am healed. I believe I am healed." Then one day, when the plant comes up, when the condition disappears, I can say, "Praise God, I am healed!" You have to have faith and tenacity to stay with it — just like the farmer does.

A long time passes before the farmer actually sees any results of his planting, but he has already made preparations for where he will store his crops. He is preparing the trucks and the reaping machines. WHY? Because he is expecting a crop to come out of that ground! He planted good seed and that is good ground and there is something built into the seed that will produce a harvest. He has done his part and he is expecting. YOU ought to expect! Glory be to God.

The exciting thing about this crop — if you ever learn to plant right and water right — is that planting of the Word of God into your life by the confession of your mouth will produce a daily harvest and not a seasonal one. Once you get the seed in the ground, keep it there, water it, feed it, and stay with it. Once it starts producing, it produces a crop every day. That is the exciting part about it.

My philosophy is this: You might as well plant, because time is going to pass anyway, even if you do not do anything. You could not be any worse off, so you cannot do anything but win!

Deuteronomy 28:14:

And thou shalt not go aside from any of the words which I command thee this day, to the right hand, or to the left, to go after other gods to serve them.

He *commands* you to do His Words — commands and *words of God* mean the same thing. God's words are commands, they are never suggestions. So, do not get hung up on just the Ten Commandments, because God told us more than ten things to do!

You Are An Heir Of God!

Galatians 4:6,7:

And because ye are sons, God hath sent forth the Spirit of his Son into your hearts, crying, Abba, Father.

Wherefore thou art no more a servant, but a son; and if a son, then an heir of God through Christ.

How much does God have? EVERYTHING! Well, you are an heir of God through Christ, so you should have everything you need and then some. So, stop belittling yourself. Stop listening to the lie of the enemy through the system, telling you how inferior you are, how homely you are, how ugly you are, how pretty you are, how handsome you are. You do not need them to tell you who you are. Let God tell you who you are.

Your feet are too big. God did not say they were too big. Your nose is too big. God never said your nose was too big. Do not let these people tell you that junk! You tell them your nose is perfect, functional and does everything God ordained it to do.

I am a son of God. I am not a slave of God. I am not chattel. I am a son, and because I am a son, I AM AN HEIR OF GOD. I love it! And think about it; Jesus has already died, so the inheritance is NOW! Our inheritance is not waiting for us in heaven. The inheritance is in this life, NOW!

Understand this, you are not a son of God just because you go to church. You are not a son of God just because you came up in what is called, "a Christian home." You are only a son of God if you have personally and individually — on your own, by an act of your will — exercised the degree of faith that you had in Jesus Christ as being the Son of God and believing in your heart that God raised Him from the dead, and accepted and confessed Him as the Lord of your life. That is what makes you a son of God.

9

#2 — Where We Are In Christ

The second thing we must learn to confess in order to live the victorious Christian life is WHERE WE ARE IN CHRIST. This refers to our position or our standing with Christ. You have probably heard people say, "How do you stand with So-and-so?" But the important question is "How do you stand with God?"

It is easy to flippantly say, "I am a son of God." That is great and that is true, but what does it really mean in terms of the everyday life that we have to live? What is my real position? Or, do I have a position? What is my standing? Or is it just, "I am going to miss hell when I die and go to heaven," and that is it? The rest of the time, we just struggle through and make it the best way we can.

Unfortunately, that is the mentality of the average Christian. It was my mentality for years. The churches that I went to did not tell me any better. They just said, "Hold on. Hang in there. Keep a stiff upper lip. Keep sending up timber every day, trying to get ready to put on my long white robe." That was about it, as far as how to deal with life.

We do have a position, a standing in Christ, and we need to know what it is. Many Christians are living a life of oppression, defeat, and fear, at the hands of Satan, our enemy, simply because they do not know their position in Christ. They do not know how they really stand with God.

You should be just as sure about where you stand with God and with Christ as you are about your own name. Now you know a person has a really serious problem if they do not know their name. Most Christians believe they have been crucified with Christ, because they have heard that all their Christian life. And that is true.

Paul says in Galatians 2:20:

I am crucified with Christ: nevertheless I live; yet not I, but Christ liveth in me: And the life which I now live in the flesh I live by the faith of the Son of God, who loved me, and gave himself for me.

Paul says, "I am crucified with Christ." That is called "identification," and it belongs to every child of God. God saw us identified with Christ. When Jesus died at Calvary, Fred Price died at Calvary. When Jesus went into the grave, Fred Price went into the grave. When Jesus rose from the dead after three days and three nights, Fred Price rose from the dead. That is how God sees me. I have to learn to see me that way.

2 Corinthians 5:14:

For the love of Christ constraineth us; because we thus judge, that if one died for all, then were all dead.

Many Christians are aware that Christ has died for them, but that still does not tell you your position. Some even dare to go another step and will believe they have risen with Christ.

Colossians 3:1:

If ye then be risen with Christ, seek those things which are above, where Christ sitteth on the right hand of God.

That, again, is identification. We have risen with Christ. But that still does not tell me my present-day position with Christ.

Even though crucified, died, and risen, you still have multitudes of Christians who are defeated in life, and that is where the rubber meets the road. If all you believe is not affecting your daily existence, then what good is it?

Because just to talk about going to heaven, you are talking about something that is abstract and nebulous. The only conscious life you really know is this one. I believe in heaven. By faith I take what the Bible says about it, but I have never experienced it yet.

We have to understand that not only were we crucified with Christ, not only did we die with Jesus, not only did we rise with Christ, but the most important thing, we *ascended* with Christ.

Ephesians 1:19-21:

> **And what is the exceeding greatness of his power to us-ward who believe** (underline the words, *greatness of his power to us-ward*. If you are a believer, then His power has been committed to you.), **according to the working of his mighty power,**
>
> **Which he wrought in Christ, when he raised him from the dead, and set him at his own right hand in the heavenly places,**
>
> **Far above all principality, and power** (the word *power* means "authority"), **and might, and dominion, and every name that is named, not only in this world, but also in that which is to come.**

When God says this about Jesus, He is talking about Fred. He is talking about *you*! As you read verse 21 over and over, you will begin to see and appreciate the enormity of this great privilege that we have.

The word *principality* in that verse refers to angelic beings of all ranks — angels, archangels, seraphim, cherubim; no matter who they are, we are above them in Christ. And the word *power* is the Greek word for "authority." We are above all authority, except, of course, God Himself. We are above the authority that Satan has in this earth realm, even though we still live here. We are above all the might, which means "strength," of Satan, demons, or anyone else. *Dominion* means "rulership," or "control." If you can get a picture of that in your heart, you will kick the devil in his backside and get him out of your business.

If any business on this planet and in this society should succeed, it ought to be your business — providing you know what you are doing. If you do not know all you need to know, ask God for wisdom. The Bible says that **Christ has been made unto us wisdom.** But you ought to succeed.

Paul says, **We are far above every name that is named.** Is fear a *name?* Then we are above fear. Is poverty a name? Then we are above poverty. Is welfare a name? Then we are above welfare. Is cancer a name? Then we are far above cancer. Is sickness a name? Is disease a name? Then we are far above them. So, you should not tolerate it! You should not permit it!

Yes, it will try to come against you. But you should stand in front of it and say, "Wait a minute! Whoa! I have ascended with Christ!" How much sickness affects Jesus? If you are seated together in heavenly places in Christ, then it should not affect *you.* Satan — the enemy and the delivery man, who brings the sickness and disease to you, will try to intimidate you by putting thoughts in your mind and getting you to confess them and own them as yours. But death and life are in the power of the tongue. You can control it.

I believe there is a place in God where we can walk above the circumstances. He says *Far above every name that is named. . . .* We win!

Ephesians 2:5:

> **Even when we were dead in sins, hath quickened** (which means "made alive") **us together with Christ, (by grace ye are saved).**

So when Jesus was made alive, we were made alive. God saw us made alive. When Christ was raised, Fred was raised! Do you see the importance of that statement? Are you going to accept defeat? Are you going to let the circumstances whip your head? Are you going to let the system tell you what you can achieve in this life? Oh, no!

Read that scripture again: It says, *And hath raised us up together, and made us sit together in the welfare office.* No, wait! Read it again: *And hath raised us up together, and made us sit together in the junk yard; in the Goodwill store; in that place where they sell day old bread.* We cannot afford fresh bread, we have to get day old, left over bread, right?

That is the mentality that many have. They let the system dictate to them and say, "That is all, you should not have any more than that." But that should not be so, because you have been raised together with Christ. You are seated together with Him in heavenly places. And you have ascended with Jesus.

How Do You Defeat the Enemy?

Think about this: God has not called us to contend with Satan *for* a place *of* victory, which we already have in Christ. I am not going into the squared circle and put the gloves on to find out who is champion. I am going into the squared circle because I AM THE CHAMPION. Knowing that you are a champion makes a difference. Your whole attitude is different. WE ALREADY HAVE THE VICTORY. We do not have to go somewhere and get it, we have it now, but we will never experience it unless we begin to confess victory and see ourselves victorious and then act victorious.

You have to get a new vision of who you are. I am a winner. I am a victor. I am a champion. I AM ON TOP. I AM THE HEAD, *NOT* THE TAIL. This principle does not only work in the area of "things," it works in every area, even husband/wife relationships. You ought to have a tranquil, peaceful, blessed, loving, sexually fulfilling, emotionally fulfilling, spiritually fulfilling relationship with your spouse. Each morning you wake up, it should not be, "Oh No! She's up again! Let me get away from this woman!" Unfortunately, that is the way many Christians do.

The Church world as a whole has not done what Jesus said, which is, "Feed my sheep and feed my lambs." Churches, for the most part, have been entertaining people. This is particularly true of black churches. I have to say that, because I have not been privileged to worship in the Hispanic, the Asian, or the Caucasian churches over a protracted period of time. But I have been in black churches for years, and I am telling you it is pathetic. The worship service is mostly *emotional* entertainment, geared to stimulating an emotional feeling, rather than imparting information.

The churches should give you the wisdom of God, show you who you are, show you what you have, show you what you can do, and not just give you a "feeling."

Many churches present either emotionalism or the other extreme of strictly *intellectualism*. In those settings, it is so quiet you can hear a pin drop on carpet, and still you have not learned anything. You hear such things as, "God is mind. God is the great universal spirit." Big deal! How does that help you pay bills? How does that destroy that 105 degree temperature in your child before brain damage occurs?

Let us find out how we can be victorious over Satan, beginning with Luke 10:17:

> **And the seventy returned again with joy, saying, Lord, even the devils** (demons) **are subject unto us through thy name.**

This is an absolutely astounding revelation. Jesus had commissioned these men to 1), go out at His behest and do some work for Him; 2), go ahead of Him into cities that

He would later go to Himself. He gave them a special dispensation of authority and told them to *heal the sick, raise the dead, cast out demons, freely ye have received, freely give.* And they went out. They were not born-again, Spirit-filled Christians at that time. They were just disciples, followers of Jesus, yet they came back with joy.

I wonder how much authority do we who are blood-bought, blood-washed, and Spirit-filled have over the demons. We, the sons of God, whose names are written in the Lamb's Book of Life, who have the sword of the Spirit, the written Word of God ought to be coming in every day with JOY instead of sadness and heaviness.

Luke 10:18,19:

And he said unto them, I beheld Satan as lightning fall from heaven.

Behold, I give unto you POWER to tread on serpents and scorpions, and over ALL the power of the enemy: and nothing shall by any means hurt you.

That is how you can defeat the enemy. That is how you can go into the squared circle as a champion and defeat *any* opponent, demonized or otherwise, that comes against you, because you have been delegated authority by Jesus Christ, the Head of the Church!

Look at Verse 19 again. I think it is awesome when He says, **nothing shall by** *any means* **hurt you.** There is not a means in existence that can hurt you! I can tell you exactly what happened in a lot of your heads as you read those words. Experiences returned to your mind, and you began remembering people you believe were real good Christians. You even began to think about your own life, and how many times you have been hurt.

But wait a minute! How long have you been confessing that you have risen with Christ? That you have ascended with Him? And that you are seated at the right hand of the Father? How long have you been speaking words of life to your life, instead of words of death? How long have you been saying with your mouth that you are a champion and that you are a victor? You have not been doing that. *That* is why you have been *hurt*. You did not know. You cannot take advantage of what you do not know.

The devil does not play fair. He does not care that you do not know. In fact, he likes it better when you do not know, so that he can, without impunity, whip your head, kick your backside, step on your toes, and push you over.

I am here to tell you that if what we have read is not true, then Jesus lied to us. But, thank God, He did not! He said, **Behold, I give unto you power. . . .** In the King James Bible, the English word *power* is used twice in Verse 19. But in the Greek, they are two entirely different words. The way it is used first is the word, *exousia*, which means "authority," "right," or "privilege." So, in reality, Jesus said, "Behold, I give unto you *authority*, *right*, or *privilege* over all the enemy's ability." I like it!

It does not matter how big the ability is. When you are the one in authority, ability is irrelevant and immaterial. If you have a General who is just 4 feet 5 inches tall, he can command the guy who is 6 feet 7 inches. It is not your size. Do not look at yourself in your own eyes. Look at yourself through the eyes of God. You are a giant in His eyes.

Confess Luke 10:19 daily. You need to say it out loud, not necessarily to your friends or relatives, because they will think you have gone stark raving mad. You can say it out loud while you are driving in your car, when you are behind closed doors, in your garage, in the pantry. You need to say it out loud so that your *own ears* can hear it. FAITH COMETH BY HEARING AND HEARING, AND HEARING, AND HEARING, AND HEARING, AND HEARING!

Keep telling yourself you are a giant, based on the Word of God. I am not talking about a psych job; I am talking about what God said about us. God cannot lie, so that is who I am. A giant. If you keep saying it, confessing it, you will finally get to the point where you will begin to believe, *"That* is who I am. I AM SOMEBODY." And you will become bold in the things of God instead of timid and easily intimidated. You will become the intimidator to the demons. And when morning time comes and the alarm clock rings, all the demons in hell will say, "Oh, NO! Fred's up again! Look out, he is up again!'

After His resurrection, but prior to going back to heaven to sit down at right hand of the Majesty on high, Jesus said in Matthew 28:18:

> ...**All power** (authority, all right or privilege) **is given unto me in heaven and in earth.**

I have shown you two scriptures that say all authority is given unto me. How much of it? All of it. That leaves nothing out. What do you suppose that all power in heaven and in earth was given to Him for? To use it! Can you agree with that?

Matthew 28:19,20:

> **Go ye therefore** (He says this based on what He said in Verse 18 — that all power has been given), **and teach all nations, baptizing them in the name of the Father, and of the Son, and of the Holy Ghost:**
>
> **Teaching them to observe all things whatsoever I have commanded you: and, lo, I am with you always, even unto the end of the world.**

After Jesus made this statement, what happened? He left. Where did He leave to? He went back to heaven. That has been 1900 years ago. Now tell me how much time has Jesus Christ spent on this planet since then? *None!* Where has He been? At the right hand of the Father. Where is that? Heaven!

But wait a minute, He said, "All power, authority, has been given unto me in *heaven* and in *earth*." He has not been here on the earth. What good does the authority do Him?

He has not been here, but when He left here and went back to heaven, He left His Body, the Church. He empowered the Church to exercise the authority here in this earth realm while He exercises the authority in the heavenly realm. He delegated all the power to the Church in the earth.

If we have all the power, what are we doing defeated? What are we doing sick, whipped and beat down? Why are we going with our needs unmet when we have all the power, all the authority? It does not make sense. It is because we have not understood *where we are*. We have not understood our position in Christ.

The ball is in our court! Whatever we bind on earth is bound in heaven, whatever we loose on earth is loosed in heaven. The opposite is also true — whatever we do not bind on earth will *not* be bound in heaven, and whatever we do *not* loose on earth will not be loosed in heaven.

My little finger has as much authority as my nose. My nose has as much authority as my foot, because my foot is as much Fred Price as my head is. Well, we are the Body of Christ. The head is no more Jesus than the feet are. Jesus is Jesus, the head is Jesus, but so is the body.

We do not have to go somewhere and contend with Satan for a place of victory. We already have it because it has been given to us. He delegated the authority to us in this earth realm by the power of attorney, ratified by the High Court of heaven. And we have the right to use His name to transact business in His absence and the Court will recognize it. When I sign the name of Jesus, the High Court of heaven will back it up, and every demon in hell has to understand and bow his knee, because I am a channel of God.

That is where we are. That is our position in Him. We are victors. All of Christ's victory is our victory!

You have all authority, authority within the boundaries of God's Word. We have to take our authority, because we do have an enemy, Satan. We do have opposition, and that opposition does not want us to operate in that authority. He wants to contain us, quarantine us, and render us inoperative.

God will not honor meaningless ritualism.

Amos 5:21,22

I hate, I despise your feast days, and I will not smell in your solemn assemblies.

Though ye offer me burnt offerings and your meat offerings, I will not accept them: neither will I regard the peace offerings of your fat beasts.

The thing that is so tragic is that, traditionally, the church has played right into the hands of the enemy. It has bogged the people down in traditions, in ritualistic precepts, rather than the Word of the living God, and God will not honor precepts. God will not honor traditions. God will not honor ritualism. God will not honor theology. I am sorry, He will not do it. You have no scripture to support it.

But I do have scripture to support what Jesus said in Matthew 28 — **All power is given unto me in heaven and in earth;** In Mark 16:17 — **And these signs shall follow them that believe;** *In my name* — that is delegated authority. **In my name....** Understand, we do not do it in our name, we do it in His name and He ratifies it. He says "Yea" and "Amen" to it, because He is not here, but we are, we are His Body. So, "what we do, He do(es)." It is the same as though He were here and did it Himself. That is how God sees it.

These Signs *Shall Follow....*

To my understanding, the strongest affirmative statement that you can make in English is, "I WILL" or "I

SHALL" do thus and so. Jesus said, **And these signs shall follow them that believe.** It does not say *may follow*. Right away, you are alerted to the fact that if *these* signs do not follow — whatever those signs are — then it means we are not believing. If the signs are not following me, and I say I believe, then I lied. Either I am a liar or Jesus is a liar.

And what are the signs that follow them that believe, according to Mark 16:17? (1)...IN MY NAME SHALL THEY CAST OUT DEVILS. In the King James Bible, it says devils, but actually there is only one devil. The word should be demons. You cannot cast out a demon if you do not believe there are such things as demons. And many in the Church world do not believe in evil spirits, but Jesus believes in evil spirits. Do you think you are smarter than Jesus? (2)...THEY SHALL SPEAK WITH NEW TONGUES.... The word *tongue* in the Greek is the word "glossa," or "glosse." The English word, *glossolalia*, comes from it and it refers to languages. It is not talking about a sinner who used to use profanity cleaning up his language and now uses nice words. It refers to speaking with other languages than those that you have learned. It is talking about the same thing that the Apostle Paul talked about in 1 Corinthians 12, 13, and 14. It is the same thing talked about in Acts 8, 10, and 19. My friend, that is Bible.

You say you believe? "Oh, yes, hallelujah, I believe." You are a liar if you do not speak with other tongues. He said, **These signs shall follow them that** *believe.* You say you believe, but you do not speak with other tongues. Either you lied or Jesus lied. Now, who do you want to believe lied?

Notice that the latter part of that 17th verse said, *they shall.* It did not say, "they might;" it did not say, "some will and some will not." It said they that believe *shall speak.* "We do not believe in speaking with tongues." If you do not believe in speaking with tongues, you do not believe in the Bible. Mark 16:17 are the words of Jesus Christ, not Fred Price.

(3) **THEY SHALL TAKE UP SERPENTS....** This is not talking about going up on the Ozarks somewhere playing with rattlesnakes to prove whether you have faith or not. This is talking about being accidentally bitten by a viper. We have a biblical account of this, when on the Island of Melita, Paul picked up that bundle of sticks and a viper grabbed his hand. He shook it off in the fire and it did not bother him in the least.

Mark 16:18:

> **They shall take up serpents; and if they drink any deadly thing, it shall not hurt them** (that means that if you drink or eat some contaminated water or food, without knowing it, you can claim your immunity. You have protection); **they shall lay hands on the sick, and they shall recover.**

Do they lay hands on the sick in your church? If they do not, your church does not believe. The only thing that would exonerate you and your church from laying hands on the sick is there are no sick people in your congregation. But *that*, you will never find!

If God wants the believers to lay hands on the sick, then it is obvious that He does not want the healthy to be sick. That proves that divine healing is for us today. If God's will is for us to be sick, He would never offer a way out of the sickness by laying hands on the sick by them that believe.

During all the years I was in the Baptist church, they never prayed for the sick. And they never preached any sermons, or taught, on healing. The only thing I ever heard relative to sickness, disease, and healing, was that Christians do not get healed anymore. I was told that all of the healings ceased when the last apostle died. The sad thing about it was, the church was full of sick people. I was one of them.

127

If it is true that these signs shall follow them that believe, then why is it that they do not pray for the sick in your church? What is wrong with the denominational church world as a whole if it does not lay hands on the sick?

To further illustrate the principle of WHERE WE ARE IN CHRIST or, our position in Christ, let us look at the story referred to as the prodigal son in Luke 15:11-31:

> And he said, A certain man had two sons:
>
> And the younger of them said to his father, Father, give me the portion of goods that falleth to me. And he divided unto them his living.
>
> And not many days after the younger son gathered all together, and took his journey into a far country, and there wasted his substance with riotous living.
>
> And when he had spent all, there arose a mighty famine in that land; and he began to be in want.
>
> And he went and joined himself to a citizen of that country; and he sent him into his fields to feed swine.
>
> And he would fain have filled his belly with the husks that the swine did eat: and no man gave unto him.
>
> And when he came to himself, he said, How many hired servants of my father's have bread enough and to spare, and I perish with hunger!
>
> I will arise and go to my father, and will say unto him, Father, I have sinned against heaven, and before thee,
>
> And am no more worthy to be called thy son: make me as one of thy hired servants.
>
> And he arose, and came to his father. But when he was yet a great way off, his father saw him, and had compassion, and ran, and fell on his neck, and kissed him.
>
> And the son said unto him, Father, I have sinned against heaven, and in thy sight, and am no more worthy to be called thy son.

But the father said to his servants, Bring forth the best robe, and put it on him; and put a ring on his hand, and shoes on his feet:

And bring hither the fatted calf, and kill it; and let us eat, and be merry:

For this my son was dead, and is alive again; he was lost, and is found. And they began to be merry.

Now his elder son was in the field: and as he came and drew nigh to the house, he heard musick and dancing.

And he called one of the servants, and asked what these things meant.

And he said unto him, Thy brother is come; and thy father hath killed the fatted calf, because he hath received him safe and sound.

And he was angry (Now there are some people who get angry with the Fred Prices of the ministry, because we talk about prosperity, victory, and faith. They are brothers, elder brothers, but they get angry.), and would not go in: therefore came his father out, and entreated him.

And he answering said to his father, Lo, these many years do I serve thee, neither transgressed I at any time thy commandment: and yet thou never gavest me a kid, that I might make merry with my friends:

But as soon as this thy son was come, which hath devoured thy living with harlots, thou hast killed for him the fatted calf.

I call your attention to the next few words. God forbid that they should be words which apply to you.

And he said unto him, (that is, the father said unto him) Son, thou art ever with me, and all that I have is thine.

Similarly, it does not matter that one boy's name was Baptist, and one boy's name was Presbyterian. That does not make any difference. You are still in the family. Verse

31 is saying, "Son, you are ever with me. But you never asked for this. You never acknowledged that you were self-righteous. You never acknowledged that you needed some help."

Unfortunately, too many people are like the elder son. Instead of asking, they have been going around as spokesmen for God, telling people what God will and will not do and have nothing to back it up scripturally. That is what religion has done.

God's Word says that the Lord is good and His mercy endureth forever — *not* until the last apostle dies.

The scripture says that the father ran out and met the boy before the boy ever arrived at the house. The awesome fact is, the father could not go out and meet the son unless the son was on his way back. And God cannot come out and meet you unless you are willing to come back. Come back from religion, tradition and ritualism.

"Son, you are ever with me. You can have everything you want."

Many Christians are like that angry son. We are sitting in the midst of plenty, yet starving to death. But that one son finally realized, "Here I am starving to death and my father's servants have more to eat than I have. I will arise and go to my father and TELL HIM I MESSED UP. I BLEW IT. I SINNED. I FAILED. I do not ask you to take me back as your son, just take me back as one of your hired servants, because they are doing well. Just let me be your servant, and I will be happy with that. It is better than what I have here in this pigpen." In spite of that, the father was waiting for him to return.

You have a position in Jesus and do not know it. You are a winner and do not know it. You are the head and not the tail, and do not know it, and do not have enough biblical sense to find out about it.

The father told his son, **You are ever with me. Everything I have is yours.** That is what the heavenly Father is saying to us.

Remember, victory will never be yours until you begin to confess that it is *yours*. Say this out loud: "Victory will never be mine until I begin to confess it as mine." It is *yours!* But there are guidelines that must be observed in order for you to get it. For instance, the boy had to come out of the pigpen. Many of you are still in the pigpen of life. You have to come out of the pigpen. You cannot be victorious if you are going to live in the pigpen!

You have to get your mind renewed with the Word. You may have to separate yourself from some people you have been associating with. You may have to leave some geographical environments that you have been in. You have to make a change, you have to decide what you want — pigpen or *victory*?

While we are dealing with this story, let me further illustrate the principle of the power of positive confession. Remember, **death and life are in the power of the tongue.** In other words, in *our* words.

Look at Verse 14-19 again:

> **And when he had spent all, there arose a mighty famine in that land; and he began to be in want.**
>
> **And he went and joined himself to a citizen of that country; and he sent him into the fields to feed swine.**
>
> **And he would fain have filled his belly with the husks that the swine did eat: and no man gave unto him.**
>
> **And when he came to himself,** *he said* (death and life are in the power of the tongue!), **How many hired servants of my father's have bread enough and to spare, and I perish with hunger!**

It does not say he *thought*. It says *he said* something. What did he say?

I will arise and go to my father, and will say unto him, Father, I have sinned against heaven, and before thee,

And am no more worthy to be called thy son: make me as one of thy hired servants.

And what did he do next? Did he remain in the pigpen the rest of his life? NO! *He arose, and came to his father!* He did something. You have to back up your mouth with your *life!* YOUR LIFE HAS TO CORRESPOND TO YOUR MOUTH, AND THEN, WHAT YOUR MOUTH SAYS WILL BECOME A REALITY IN YOUR LIFE. YOU HAVE TO *DO* SOMETHING!

You can arise today. I do not care where you are. I do not care if you are in the pigpen of life. I do not care if you are feeding swine, you can come out of that place, but you will have to arise. You will have to come to yourself and make a confession. You have to come to yourself and speak life to your life.

You have to say, "What am I doing wasting my life here? I am a child of the King! I have been born again, and filled with the Holy Ghost. I have been living below my privileges. I have been letting the devil dictate the terms of my life, and I am going to arise and go to my Father." How do you do that? You do it with the WORD! That is your right and privilege. That is the privilege you have in Christ.

10

#3 — What We Possess in Christ

We must confess WHAT WE POSSESS IN CHRIST if we are to live the overcoming and victorious life that Christ came to bring us. This has to deal with our inheritance. Whether you realize it or not, as a child of God, you have an inheritance. You have something that was left to you by a very rich person.

If you are poor, you usually do not leave a will, because you have nothing to bequeath to anyone. You do not need to spend money getting an attorney that deals with wills and estates when you have none. When you leave a will, it means you have something that you want disposed of after your demise, and you specifically want it to go to your heirs.

Well, Jesus Christ left a will. In fact, it is the book we call the Bible. The New Testament is actually the last will and testament of the Lord Jesus Christ. It is a legal document ratified by the High Court of Heaven, and Jesus is the executive administrator of the will. But He cannot execute the will if the heirs do not cooperate. And the heirs cannot cooperate if the heirs do not know they *are* heirs. If they do not know they have an inheritance, how can they claim it? How are you going to benefit from it when you do not know you have one?

Satan keeps most Christians in bondage to some degree at least, and whips their heads and kicks their backsides, because they do not know they have, and they do not claim, their inheritance. He did mine for years. I thought my head was a punching bag! He whipped me every way but loose! And I thought God was doing it.

The churches that I went to said the Lord was doing that, and because I did not know I had an inheritance, I could not claim it. I ended up struggling, walking the streets of my city without a job, could not pay my bills, could not take care of my family, and I thought it was all a part of what was normal as a Christian.

Again, I did not know I had an inheritance. We need to recognize that we do have an inheritance. If we do not, Satan is going to steal everything we have. He is going to usurp our rights and privileges, and leave us on welfare — he has been doing that to vast multitudes of Christians.

I am going to say something that will be considered controversial in the traditional church world, but I challenge *you* to challenge your own minister with what I am going to say. You do not have to believe anything I say, but you ask your minister and watch his face, his expression, his eyes, when you start asking him some of these things that I am going to tell you to ask him. Tell him not to give you a lot of "mumbo-jumbo," a lot of theological yuk, yuk, yuk. You ask him to show you in the Book, chapter and verse, in English, that what I am going to say is not true. But do not just take his word, and do not just take mine. You should be able to read it for yourself.

I am going to give you scripture for what I am about to tell you: We have an inheritance. A part of your inheritance is that you do not have to be sick.

When I go back in my mind, I remember people I knew who loved the Lord — and I am not talking about the elderly, I am speaking of people in the prime of life who died of debilitating diseases — because they did not know they had an inheritance, guaranteeing them divine healing and health. The devil took advantage of them, of their ignorance of their inheritance and stole it from them. And I watched those people die.

But just because somebody died does not mean that was God's will. You cannot use that rationale, because if you do, you would have to say that it is God's will when somebody dies unsaved and goes to hell. And that is not God's will. The Bible says that it is not God's will that **...any should perish, but that all should come to repentance.** The Bible did not say that God gave His Son because He so loved a *certain segment* of humanity. No! The Bible says, for God so loved *the world* that He gave His only begotten Son. However, there is a qualifier: **that whosoever believeth in Him should not perish.**

If you do not take advantage of your inheritance, that is not God's fault. He provided it for you. But Satan, if given the chance, will steal from you. He will steal your health. He will steal your well-being, your family, your children, your wife, your husband.

Part of your inheritance is divine health. The ultimate goal is divine health, not divine healing. Divine healing is simply a pathway to divine health. God's best is health, not healing. Thank God for the healing that can catapult you into the health, but the best is to walk in health and not need to be healed. But you cannot take advantage of your inheritance if you do not know it. Then, even if you know it, you have to confess it as yours. Yes, confess it right in the midst of the 105 degree temperature.

I am NOT telling you not to go to the doctor. I am saying that in order to activate your covenant, you have to confess it. In the final analysis, it is still God Who has to do the miraculous part. For instance, if you break a bone, the doctor cannot make that bone grow together. He can set it, but then he has to step back after he has put the cast on, fold his arms and wait for something beyond any of our ability to comprehend, to do its job.

God wants you well. We can be healed and then learn how to cooperate with the things that God has set in motion, eat the right things, take care of our body and not give the devil place. The Bible says *give the devil no place.* That means you have to take care of yourself; otherwise, you will give him a place. You cannot beat your body to death and expect it to work. When you do that, you open the door for the enemy to come in like a flood. But if you do what you are supposed to do, you can minimize the attacks of Satan in terms of those attacks having any affect on you. You have to deal with the attacks, because they are going to come. You are in an environment that is surrounded by negative forces, but you can flick them off — like you do flies!

I will wager that every one of you has known someone who was a Christian who died before their time. When I say, before their time, I mean before they were 70 years old. God said, **My people are destroyed for a lack of knowledge** (Hos.4:6). We need to know what our inheritance is.

We have a right to healing. We have a right to health. We have a right to joy. We have a right to peace. Those things have been provided for you, but you have to know it and appropriate it by *faith.* The way you do that is by a combination of 1) confessing it, saying it, speaking it, and 2) by buttressing that up with a lifestyle which corresponds to what you say with your mouth. Can you understand that?

In most of our churches, most of the theology is futuristic. It is all about what we are going to get in the future, over there on the other side, in the sweet by and by. But I am here to tell you that according to the Word of God, you can have the sweet *now* and *now,* and the sweeter *by* and *by!* That is what you possess as a child of God.

If you read the four Gospels, it is very interesting to note that Jesus did not come down here and encase Himself in a plastic bubble and have His disciples roll Him along for 3½ years up and down the roads of Palestine. You read time and time again where He went into somebody's house and had a meal. In fact, He was so accustomed to doing that, the religious leaders said, "He eats with publicans and sinners." In fact, He got a reputation as wine bibber because He was always with people.

In other words, Jesus came down here and lived where we have to live, and the purpose of that was to show us that God is a very present help in the everyday life that we live, and not off in the future. God is interested in us *now.* That is why the Bible says of Jesus when He came, *I came to seek and to save that which was lost.*

He came down here right in the midst of us. He lived among us, walked among us, experienced the things that people went through, and was moved by it. When Lazarus died, the Bible says, Jesus wept. He was a man of compassion, and He did what He could, where He could, to alleviate the pain and misery. He did what He did to show us what can happen for us *today,* as well as for those who lived in His day.

When I found out that Jesus not only saved me from sin, but He saved me from sickness, disease, poverty, fear, and any other negative thing that would destroy me and take my life, I got mad! I got righteously indignant. I got just as mad as Jesus got when He went into the temple and made that whip and chased those moneychangers out! He told them to take the doves out of the temple, because it was His Father's house and it was supposed to be a house of prayer and they had made it a den of thieves. He whipped them out of there. That is what you call righteous indignation. Not mad where you break up the furniture and beat your wife and abuse your kids, but righteously indignant.

When I found out about my inheritance, I got mad at the church, mad at the preacher. I got mad at theology, because they lied to me. I trusted my life to them and they lied to me. I thought they could be trusted. That is why now, I only trust the Bible. I will listen to what you have to say, but you tell me where it came from so that I can check it out, because I want to be sure you know how to read. You may have read it wrongly. I cannot take any chances. MY LIFE IS AT STAKE!

All Things Are Yours

I got cheated out of seventeen years of my covenant rights. But when I found out the truth, I determined that if anybody on the planet was going to have the benefits of the inheritance, it was going to be me!

Let me give you a scriptural example of your inheritance:

1 Corinthians 3:21:

> **Therefore let no man glory in men. For all things are yours.**

Underline the words *all things*. It did not say *all spirituals*. It said, THINGS. Is an automobile a thing? Is furniture a thing? Is jewelry a thing? Are clothes things? Are houses and lands and money things? He said ALL THINGS. ALL means "everything without exception, nothing left out."

Also notice what it does not say. It does not say all things are God's. It says all things are *yours*. Paul is writing to every individual person in the family of God. We could personalize it and say all things are *mine*.

1 Corinthians 3:22:

> **Whether Paul, or Apollos, or Cephas, or the world, or life, or death, or things present, or things to come; all are yours.**

What does it mean, *Paul is mine?* Paul is mine because what? Paul did not receive the revelations that he received from God only for his personal benefit. He received those revelations from God, so that he might communicate them to the Body of Christ. In the process of communicating them, he would also get the benefit and privilege to use them if he chose to.

Likewise, it says that Apollos and Cephas are ours. They were men mightily used of God in the early church. They were used by the Spirit of God to minister to the needs of the people.

And who does the world belong to? According to 1 Corinthians 3:22, it belongs to *us!* We have been lied to. We have been told we are just victims of the circumstances. But the world belongs to us! What does that mean? Does that mean you can go out and indiscriminately grab a block of land and say, "This is mine. It belongs to me"? NO! It means that if there is anything good about it, if there is anything beneficial about it, if there is anything that would help or enhance our lives, we have a right to it. Because the world belongs to us!

Psalm 115:16 says,

The heaven, even the heavens, are the Lord's: but the earth hath he given to the children of men.

GOD CREATED THIS WORLD FOR US, HIS CHILDREN! If He gave us the earth, then everything in the earth belongs to us. And the good thing about this is that when God gives it to you, He gives it to you all the way, from the surface all the way down to the core!

We have another witness that tells us the world belongs to us:

Genesis 1:26:

And God said, Let us make man in our image, after our likeness: and let them have dominion... (Do you know what *dominion* means? It means "lordship," "rulership," "oversight," "caretakership," "ownership." It means you are in charge!) **over ALL the earth, and over every creeping thing that creepeth upon the earth.**

139

We are supposed to have dominion. That is how God created it. That is what our possession is. Not in heaven, but in *this* life.

First Corinthians 3:22 also tells us that life belongs to the child of God. It is a PRECIOUS POSSESSION. LIFE! Then it says, not only life, but DEATH is ours. Now, what does that mean? We have been led to believe, from traditional Christianity, that God is the author of death; that God may just decide to indiscriminately kill people or take them out of here.

There is no set time for you to die.

We have all heard this thing about every man has a time to die. No, he does not. You are going to die for sure, but there is no set time for you to die. God does not have some chart up in heaven with everybody's name on it and the date they are going to die, regardless of what you do or what you say. If that were true, then the Bible would be invalidated. We would have to get rid of most of the Bible, because the promises of God are not based upon the fact that God has some set time for you to die.

Because God is God, He is omniscient and knows everything, He knows *when* everybody is going to die, but He is *not responsible for them dying at that time.* Do you understand that? We *are* going to die. The Bible very clearly tells us that in Hebrews 9:27: for ...**it is appointed unto men once to die, but after this the judgment.**

So, there is an appointment that you have with death, but we have never been informed that *we* ought to make the appointment. We have been laboring under the delusion that God arbitrarily makes the appointment and there is nothing you can do about it.

As I said, if that were true, it would invalidate so much of the Bible, because there are promises and promises in the Bible that have to do with our choice about how long we live, not on God. For instance, part of the 91st Psalm says, **With long life will I satisfy him, and shew him my salvation.** (Who will be satisfied?) *He that dwelleth in the secret place of the Most High and abides under the shadow of the Almighty.* What is long life? Long life is *not* 35 years, friend, or 16 years, or 8 years. That is *not* long life.

God also said, **Honor thy father and mother that thy days may be long upon the land which the Lord thy God giveth thee.** Why would He hold out a promise like that to me, then take me out at 25? He would be lying to me. He said, **With long life....** But if you do not know that you have life and death, if you do not know that you have something to do with it, you drop your guard and assume that it is inevitable. You allow fate to do its work and without realizing it, Satan operates within those confines and comes against you and destroys you. Then we end up blaming God for it.

God is not taking anybody with death. He has never taken anybody that way. There are only three people God ever took. All of the places in the Bible which says God had anything to do with the person leaving, God took them *alive.* And the only three we have any record of God taking were Enoch, Elijah, and Jesus. They all left here *alive, not dead.* LIFE IS YOURS AND SO IS DEATH!

God Shall Supply Your Need

Many people have reduced God down to the level of some supercosmic idea and believe that everything out there is in "star trek land." But God is very, very interested in what you will be experiencing in the practical issues of your day-to-day life. God is the God of the ALL.

Philippians 4:19:

> **But my God shall supply all your need according to his riches** (not my poverty, not my empty wallet, and not my empty bank account) **in glory** (How?) **by Christ Jesus.**

So, if God supplies *all* your needs, that means none of your needs are left out, right? You do not have any needs. Many people do not understand that and say, "I am not going to give Fred Price any money because he does not have any needs." But they have missed the point altogether. They do not understand that what I am doing when I confess, "I believe that all my needs are met," is exactly what God says. And that is what causes the needs to come to be met.

The scripture does not say, "He had supplied." It said, **He shall...** That means the need cannot be met until it *becomes a need.* The only thing that God has to supply is whatever it is you *need.* If you do not need it yet, God does not have to supply it yet, because there is nothing to supply.

When I confess that all my needs are met, I am saying that by faith. Remember, I am talking about a *lifestyle* of faith. Romans 1:17 says, ...**The just shall live by faith.** It is a life lived every minute of every hour of every second of every day of every week of every month of every year of every decade. It is not an isolated situation kind of thing. It is a *total* lifestyle. You cannot go on "flights" — operating by faith today, and not operating by faith tomorrow.

I have been operating by faith for nearly 20 years, and I have not yet attained the plateau that I am planning to attain. I have been believing this and teaching this and confessing this for nearly 20 years. I have not reached the top yet. But because of practicing this principle of positive confession all the time, I have come to a place in my life where I actually have no unmet needs. For years now, I have only been dealing with desires.

But Psalm 37:4 says,

Delight thyself also in the Lord; and he shall give thee the desires of thine heart.

Some people might say, "I'm not gonna give him anything, 'cause he said he don't have no needs." But wait a minute, do not deny me my *desires*. I do have some desires! Help me with the desires. *Needs*, that is not all there is to life.

When I did not have a dollar in my pocket, I said, "Praise God, my God supplies all my need according to His riches in glory by Christ Jesus." Understand that it is not true because you have it. It is true because God said it. Because God said it and you believe and confess it, that is what produces it. That is what causes it to come to pass.

The scripture did not say that my God shall supply all my need, when I can figure out how God is going to do it. It says, **My God *shall* supply. . . .** I have to believe that and confess it. When I confess it, put action to it, that is my faith talking, and that opens the channel for God.

God can show Himself mighty once He has a channel. But if you limit Him by trying to figure out with your little pea-sized brain how He is going to do it, then you will limit Him, and He will not be able to do it. I have been speaking life to my life for nearly 20 years, and it has been building up reserves. That is how it works, it builds up. And so, as it builds up, you end up with an abundance past your needs.

Then you get to the point where you become the "need meeter" for other people, because, ultimately, all needs are met through people. It does not fall out of the sky. I have never, personally, received any money from out of the sky. None. And neither have you! Every dollar that has come to me has been because some human was around somewhere. But it was God speaking to them, directing them, because of my faith.

For example, God meets the needs of the local church that I pastor through the obedience of the people who tithe and give offerings. No money has fallen out of the sky in all the years I have been pastor of Crenshaw Christian Center. It all comes through the offerings.

In the natural, it is crazy to give away money you have worked for. Yet you give it to God and you cannot see Him. That is unintelligent if you look at it academically. But if you look at it spiritually, you understand what it is. People being obedient to the Word of God, and through that, God meets the needs of the congregation I pastor. That is the way He does it in your own life.

This is what you possess. You have a right to have your needs met. You have to also understand that there are some parameters that govern and control the meeting of that need. For instance, for the nearly 20 years that I have been giving, I have been paying tithes — not out of duty, but out of love, because I wanted to be obedient.

Thank God that He gave me something I could do. If He had told me to run 500 miles an hour, I would not make it. If He had told me to make straight A's on all my school tests, I would have flunked out and missed it.

If He had told me to climb to the top of Mt. Everest, I could have not done that. But He gave me something I *could* do. Give 10% of my income, and then of course, give offerings, and I gladly give it.

As I began to give, it got so good I started giving more than what He asked. Not because I felt any compunction to do it, but just because I decided I wanted to do it. I wanted to because I had cheated Him for so many years and did not give Him anything. I said, ''I want to make my amends.'' Not that I felt that I had to, or that I would feel guilty if I did not do it, but just because I could. So, I began giving away 25% of all my income.

I started operating in these spiritual laws. If you keep planting good seed in good ground and taking care of the ground, harvest is assured, because harvest is built into the seed. It is automatic, but the seed has to be planted correctly.

As I began planting seed, the harvest began coming, and that is how God supplied my needs. That is why giving is so important. You not only have to confess the Word, but you have to *do* the Word. And the Word says, "Will a man rob God?" The people said, "How have we robbed You?" And God said, "In tithes and offerings." He said, "Bring ye all the tithes into the storehouse." So, you have to do that, too.

What is so peculiar to me is that people will balk at paying a 10% tithe. I mean, they get upset! "I don't see why I gotta pay a 10% tithe," they will say, but then for the privilege of using a bank card, they will pay 18% to 20% annual interest and think nothing of it! They will pay that much interest to strangers, but balk at paying their own heavenly Father 10% tithes.

Reconciling Spiritual and Material Things

According to God's Word, I am already blessed. We possess blessings, not curses, as a result of being in Christ. Blessings are part of our inheritance.

Ephesians 1:3:
Blessed be the God and Father of our Lord Jesus Christ, who hath (underline the word hath) **blessed us** (underline the word blessed) **with all** (underline the word all) **spiritual blessings in heavenly places in Christ.**

The word *h-a-t-h* means "has" and that is past tense, which indicates that the time of action has already taken place. It is not in the process of taking place. It is not going to take place someday off in the distant future. Has blessed is past tense.

According to the scripture we just read, we are blessed with *all*. . . . All is an inclusive term. No blessing is left out. Now, here is the dilemma. "It is great that I am blessed with all spiritual blessings but, Lord, my roof is leaking. That is *not* spiritual. Lord, I have bald tires on my car. The side of the tire and the tread are so thin, I can see the cord. Thank You, Lord, for blessing me spiritually, but I need some tires for my car. *That* is *material*, not spiritual. Lord, I thank You for blessing me with all spiritual blessings in heavenly places in Christ, but did You know the property tax bill just came? That is not spiritual. Lord, I need some money to pay my property taxes, and I do not have any!"

A legitimate question at this time would be, "How do you reconcile these spiritual and material things?" By going back to Jesus. Jesus is the reason. He is the fountain head of it all. Jesus is where it begins.

The question again is, "How are these spiritual blessings translated into material blessings in everyday life?" There is a simple answer. What we have to do is go back and think of things in terms of origin. We need to go back to the beginning, back to Genesis. I want to show you the process that the Spirit of God showed me so that you can understand the relationship between the spiritual and the material.

When I first was confronted by the verse in Ephesians, **Blessed be the God and Father of our Lord Jesus Christ, who hath blessed us with all spiritual blessings. . .,** I had the economic wolf on my front porch, and God was talking about *spiritual* blessings. I needed some money, honey! How does that verse translate into money? The Lord showed me how it does in Genesis 1:1: **In the beginning God created the heaven and the earth.**

Question: What are the heaven (the solar system) and the earth? Are they spiritual items or material items? Material, of course.

146

Question: Which came first, God or the earth? God, of course. Then God must be more real than the heaven and the earth He created. Right? Right!

Let us take another step towards our solution: John 4:24: **God is a Spirit....** Now look at John 1:1:

In the beginning was the Word, and the Word was with God, and the Word was God.

The word in the Greek is *logos*, and that word means ''Jesus or the Son of God, Christ, or Messiah,'' or ''second person in the Godhead.''

It said, **In the beginning....** That sounds familiar: In the beginning God.... In the beginning was the Word.... In the beginning God created.... In the beginning was the Word.

If anybody ought to know what God is, Whoever was with God in the beginning ought to know. Jesus was there and He says that God is a Spirit.

I asked you if the earth was material or spiritual, and we determined that it was material. If that is true and God created it, and Jesus said that God is a Spirit, then that means that a Spirit created material things. That means that the Spirit must be more real than the material things that He created, which means that everything that is material had its origin in the Spirit. That means that material things are dependent upon spiritual things for their existence, which means everything starts in the Spirit realm.

When the scripture says **Blessed be the God and Father of our Lord Jesus Christ, who hath blessed us with all spiritual blessings in heavenly places in Christ,** that means that the leaky roof was first of all spiritual. It means that those four bald-headed tires were first of all spiritual. It means the money I needed to pay taxes with was first of all spiritual, because it was a Spirit that created material things. Can you understand that?

So, I have my roof in Christ in heavenly places. I have my four new tires in heavenly places. I have money to pay my taxes in heavenly places. And all I have to do is believe it and by my faith bring it into the reality of the material world by my positive confession of God's Word, because it is mine. Hallelujah!

It starts in the Spirit world and by FAITH is brought into the material world. That truth is *awesome!* Let us go back to Genesis 1:1-3:

> **In the beginning God created the heaven and the earth.**
>
> **And the earth was without form, and void; and darkness was upon the face of the deep. And the Spirit of God moved upon the face of the waters.**
>
> **And God SAID, Let there be light: and there was light.**

But notice that there was no light until *after* God SAID IT. He had faith in His own words. That is why it takes faith to please God, because He is a faith God. He operates on faith.

He said, **Let there be light: and there was light.** He said, **Let the dry land appear, and the dry land appeared.** Nothing came into existence until after God SAID IT. He did it by the WORDS of His mouth. That is how He created this material world that we live in. He was using the law of confession. He was speaking it into existence. And if you want that new roof, talk it into existence.

If you want those new tires, talk them into existence. If you want the money to pay your taxes, talk it into existence. You are already blessed. You have your roof; you have your tires; you have your tax money. Just speak it into existence. It works! YOU HAVE TO SPEAK IT!

I really like what the Hebrew says about this. In the King James Version, it says, And God said, **Let there be light, and there was light.** The real essence of the Hebrew is that God said, LIGHT BE, and LIGHT WAS. I like that. ROOF BE, and ROOF WAS. Glory to God!

148

Ephesians 1:3:

Blessed be the God and Father of our Lord Jesus Christ, who hath blessed us with all spiritual blessings in heavenly places in Christ.

God has made an investment, a deposit, in Christ for us. We have to start with the spiritual and bring them, by our faith, into the physical three-dimensional world. That is why He says we are "blessed with all spiritual blessings."

According to God's Word, all of our needs are met. By faith, we must confess it, and then, of course, line up with all of the other things that God's Word declares that we ought to do. Thereafter, we can expect, absolutely, positively, unequivocally, that all of our needs will be met and manifested in due season — if we faint not, but stand on God's unchanging Word.

Fear Not

What else do we possess in Christ?

2 Timothy 1:7:

For God hath not given us the spirit of fear; but of power, and of love, and of a sound mind.

That tells us that fear is a spirit. Fear is an unnatural thing for man. God did not build us or create us with fear potential. What happened was that when Adam sinned and man died spiritually — died in the sense of being cut off from God — he was left strictly to fleshly or soulish things.

Since Satan, the god of this world, operates in the realm of the flesh and soul, he is allowed to send his demon spirits with all kinds of fears. That is what we respond to, because God has not given us the spirit of fear, because fear does not come from God.

When I say fear, I am talking about that paralyzing kind of thing that seems to come over you in given situations, where you lose contact with reality, and, in some cases, even freeze up, unable to move and become helpless. That is not of God.

I am not talking about reverential fear, or respect. For instance, I have a water heater in my house. This gas water heater has a pilot light with fire in it. I am not afraid of fire, but I have great respect for it. I know that I should not put my hands in the burner to warm them, because I could lose them.

To have respect for something is one thing, but to be so afraid that you cannot carry on daily activities is another. To go a mile out of the way to avoid a dog is unnatural and does not make sense.

Your newborn, re-created human spirit comes from God and God does not send anything down here with fear in it. So fear comes out of your soul and out of your body.

Even as a Christian, fears can come into your flesh, into your mind, and control your life. If you do not know that you have a right to do so, and you do not learn how to confess that you do not have the spirit of fear, that spirit will overtake you. You have to learn how to resist fear, just like you would resist somebody taking something away from you. You resist fear with your confession and with your stand of faith. I had to do that.

All of my life, as far as my conscious remembrance goes, I was afraid of water, afraid of it in the sense of putting my head under water. I only have little snatches of memory that something negative occurred. My father had a drinking problem, and he would get stoned, as we say, and do some crazy things.

I vaguely remember we were at the beach during a holiday. He had been drinking. He picked me up and put me on his shoulders. I was just a little fellow at the time, and my legs dangled around his neck. He started out into the water and I was petrified. I kept hollering, ''No! No! No!'' as we kept getting deeper and deeper and deeper until the water came up to where I was. I do not know whether he dropped me or whether he put me in. That part is a blank. But ever since that time, I had a fear of putting my head under the water. In fact, I could not get my head close to the water, even in the shower.

If I was taking a shower and happened to turn my head the wrong way and water went up my nose, I would begin to gag and gasp for breath. I felt smothered, or claustrophobic.

Think about it, a grown man, and I never had my head under water until I was forty years old. I would not go swimming. In fact, I used to watch Jacques Cousteau on television — I loved the undersea world and I wanted to go underwater. I thought, ''Boy, that is wonderful. What a blessing to be able to go under water and see all the undersea world that God has created.'' Then, I would begin thinking about putting my head under water and fear would start creeping all over me.

Some of you have had — or have — fears like I had. Examples: going into close places like an elevator, or going into tall buildings, or in high places. All these are fears; we call them phobias. These fears are not natural. They do not come in the genes. They are learned. These spirits can become a part of you as a child and affect you the rest of your life. But you have to overcome them with the Word of God and your faith.

I found out from God's Word that He did not give me the spirit of fear; I did not have to be afraid of anything. I made a statement one time in a sermon, that by my faith, I had overcome all the fears I ever had — except for the fear of putting my head under water. I said, ''I am going to learn how to swim. Up till now, I have not had the time to do it, and I do not have a swimming pool!''

Two members of my church heard me make that statement and offered me their swimming pool and provided me with their swimming instructor, free of charge. That made it convenient for me, and I went to their home and learned how to swim. I overcame that fear with my faith, applying God's Word to my situation.

Shortly thereafter, I had a pool put in my yard. Then I said, "I am going to learn how to scuba dive." And I became a certified scuba diver. I did the same thing with flying on airplanes.

For years, I would not fly on an airplane. You could not get me on an airplane! You could not shoot me, handcuff me, put me in a coffin and get me on an airplane! I would resurrect! I was terrified and yet I loved airplanes. That is why it is a paradox. But it was really not the fear of airplanes, it was the fear of *death*. I had to learn that the Lord had delivered me from the fear of death.

Thank God I found out that God had not given me the spirit of fear. You have to know that and confess it. It will take some time, and you will not lose that fear overnight. If you have been afraid of something for forty years, you will not lose that fear like snapping your fingers. You have to fight it, and you have to stand against it.

The Bible says, **We wrestle not against flesh and blood** (Eph. 6:18). It is a battle, a fight. It is real.

I remember one time as the pastor of a small church, I had to go to a meeting in Chicago (from Los Angeles), to represent my little pastorate. I did not have much time to get there, and there was only one practical way to go. YOU GUESSED IT. By airplane!

I had a friend, a businessman, who flew all the time. He was telling me all of the advantages of flying first class as opposed to flying coach or tourist class. He told me that his company would provide him with a coach ticket and then, for a few more dollars, he would pay the difference himself and ride first class. So, I decided to travel first class, since this was my first flight.

I went to the airport, shaking all the way there. I will not lie to you, my palms were sweaty. I was afraid, but there was nothing I could do. I had to go and I could not refuse to go without revealing how scared I really was. I had to play it cool. Here I was, leading people, telling them what to do, and I was scared myself!

I got on the plane, put my seat belt on, and sat back to await the flight. I was seated by the window on a 707 four-engine jet. Right outside my window was the right wing with two engines hanging on it.

The flight was supposed to depart at 10 o'clock. I am a very punctual person, so I assume everybody else is, too. Well, 10 o'clock came, then 10:05, then 10:10, and the plane had not moved. I was really getting nervous now. I had psyched myself up to fly, and now they were late!

All kinds of thoughts began to run through my mind as to why they were late. Finally, the captain came over the loudspeaker and said, "Ladies and gentlemen, we are experiencing a few technical difficulties."

That was all I needed to hear — something WRONG WITH THE PLANE! I thought, "You must be kidding. My first flight, and you have mechanical problems?!" My stomach was turning over on the inside. At about 10:15, the plane still had not moved. I broke out in a cold sweat. At about 10:20, the pilot came back on the intercom, "Ladies and gentlemen, we believe that we have located our problem and the mechanics will be moving towards that problem in a few moments to fix it. And we should be airborne in approximately 10 to 15 minutes. Thank you very much for your patience."

Two mechanics approached the plane with a ladder and tool box. Think about this: Here is a four-engine airplane. You have four possibilities of mechanical problems in the engines. Two engines on the right side of the plane and two engines on the left side. Why couldn't it be one of the

engines on the left side of the plane? No! It had to be one
of the engines on the right side of the plane — where I was
sitting! Of the two engines — one is called the inboard
engine and one is the outboard. The outboard engine is
camouflaged by the inboard engine. Funny thing, it would
not be a problem with the outboard engine, it was the
inboard engine — right outside my window!

The mechanics went to work, with their ladder up to
the engine, peering inside. One of the men took a
screwdriver from his tool box. I could see the engine parts
gleaming in the sunlight, like the organs of the human body!
I was thinking, the mechanic, like some famous heart
surgeon, was going to deftly insert the screwdriver into
those engine innards, like a surgeon would into the human
body. But no, he jabs it into those engine parts like he was
chipping ice with an ice pick!

Inside, I was screaming. NO! What are you doing?!
STOP! By this time, I am wiping sweat off my face. I was
absolutely petrified. FEAR WAS ALL OVER ME — God's
great man of faith and power! Finally, they finished. We
left one hour late. By this time I was totally out of it. I could
not have been more out of it if I had had 500 ounces of
heroin. I had overdosed on FEAR!

To further compound the fear, I did not know that
much about automatic pilots. Once they reach cruising
altitude, they put the plane on automatic pilot. Periodically,
the automatic pilot will make adjustments for the course
and you can feel a slight flutter or movement, especially
if you are scared like I was. I was extremely sensitive to every
move, every sound, every noise.

I was so scared, I sat in that seat with my eyes glued
to the window. And from Los Angeles to Chicago, I watched
that engine all the way! I did not take my eyes off that
engine. I was traveling first class, so the stewardesses were
coming down the aisles with those four-wheeled carts

serving prime rib of beef with all the trimmings. But I did not eat. I did not drink a Coca Cola. I was sooo terrified. I just watched that engine all the way to Chicago. Every time the plane fluttered or made a slight movement, I just knew that engine was going to fall off. But if it had, what in the world could I have done about it?! FEAR IS RIDICULOUS. It does not make sense. What could I do if the wing fell off? NOTHING! When I got to Chicago and got off that plane, I hugged the ground!

That is a true story. But by coming into the truth of God's Word, I took my faith, as I did with the fear of water, and I overcame that fear of flying. And, as of this writing, I have flown over a million miles on aircraft. As a matter of fact, I have been in some situations where it looked like the plane was going down, and I probably was the only one on board who was not afraid. No fear. None whatsoever. I took my faith and overcame.

What I have told you are real life issues. You can use this same overcoming faith on dogs. You can use it on the dark, because some of you are afraid of the dark. You can use this on staying home at night alone. You can use this overcoming faith on anything, because you have not been given the spirit of FEAR.

As a child of God, you have no legitimate reason to fear anything, because God is in you by His Holy Spirit. But you have to believe and you have to confess it. You have to say, "I BELIEVE I AM NOT AFRAID." And then, keep right on walking, and you will break that spirit. It cannot stay with you if you will confess the Word of God over that situation.

At first you may be like I was on that flight to Chicago, sweating all the way. But your faith, like mine, can say, "I believe everything is fine. I believe I am safe."

We walk by faith and not by sight — we walk by the Word of God and not by what our senses are telling us.

You have not been given the spirit of fear. You possess that in Christ. You do not have to be afraid of anything as a child of God. Now, use wisdom. If you drop a dime inside a lion's mouth, just consider the fact that you lost a dime!! Do not stick your head inside the lion's mouth. You do not do dumb things.

If you drop something in the fire, do not reach inside unless the Spirit of God tells you to — and you had better *know* that it is the Spirit of God telling you, like Shadrach, Meshach and Abednego in the Book of Daniel.

But ordinarily, you do not play around with certain things. You should have respect and use wisdom. But you do not have to be afraid and you do not have to back off of anything.

People are afraid of dogs. If you put a sign on a wall around your property that says, BEWARE, VICIOUS DOG! forget it. I am not going in. But if I am walking down the street in the direction that is the shortest distance to where I want to go, and a dog comes out, I am not going to turn around and go three miles out of the way to avoid that dog.

Let me tell you how to break your fear, that spirit that comes against your mind and against your flesh. The way you break the fear of flying is by going to the airport and getting on an airplane as soon as possible. That is the only way. You will never break it on the ground. You have to face the fear in its own element in that very place where it says you are afraid.

All of these provisions (blessings) are available to the extent that we are willing to confess that they are ours. The only way you will have those blessings in actual manifestation in your life is to confess them. That is what makes it work. "I possess this because I am in Christ. I have a covenant right to it because the Word of God says so. God says so. Jesus says so, and I say so. I do not care who says I do not, I say I do!"

The only person who can stop your blessings from coming is YOU! That is the wonderful thing about walking by faith. That is what I like about it. That is why I encourage you to learn how to walk by your own faith. Do not get into the habit of having someone else agree with you. Do not misunderstand me. It is good that husbands and wives be of one accord. They should be in agreement. But the bottom line is, this is between you and the Word of God.

I want to share with you a very precious letter as an example of what we possess in Christ. It is a good example of the power of positive confession, how someone took a stand on God's Word, made their confession, and received their heart's desire. It says:

Dear Pastor Price:

...My husband and I are new to Los Angeles and to Crenshaw. We are here because of the power of positive confession. For a number of years, while we lived in Dallas, we had studied with you. It was through your teachings that we first gained spiritual knowledge of Proverbs 18:21 and how faith works. As we studied with you and several other anointed teachers, our measure of faith was challenged in several areas, so we started putting our mustard seed faith out there. We began to change what we said. Instead of confessing every thing that was going wrong, we started saying, "Father, we thank You that Your Word does not return to You empty, but it will accomplish what pleases You and achieve the purpose for which You sent it. We thank You that all of our needs are met according to Your riches in glory by Christ Jesus. We thank You that we can do all things through Christ who strengthens us and that no weapon formed against us can prosper.''

At first, we took real baby steps, oftentimes repeating these Bible confessions right behind you as we ran the tape back and forth. But with time, our steps strengthened, and our faith grew.

We went from a seed to a bush, then to a hedge, and finally started to get the first branches on our faith tree. That brings us to Crenshaw. We had our first opportunity to fellowship at Crenshaw in July, 1984. You did not make it to Dallas that year, so we decided we could get you and Disneyland in at the same time. We arrived that Friday evening and decided we'd go spy out the church that Saturday. We would be all set for Sunday.

We drove over to the old church and saw the "Moved" sign. So, we found Vermont Avenue. I must say we were not exactly prepared for 7901 South Vermont. We thought, "Boy! If faith can do this and more, we are gonna stick with this. The security officer was so very cordial and gave us all the information we needed for Sunday morning. As we arrived for the first service, our spirits got more and more excited. Even in the perimeters of the church, we sensed something was very different. And when we actually reached the campus, we knew we were on Holy ground.

Even though we had been studying with you quite a while, we felt just like children as we sat and listened to the Word which came forth, hanging on and gobbling up every word. One of the things we had always appreciated in you is the simplicity of the Word of God delivered through you.

When I listened to you teach, I knew the truth of "For my yoke is easy and my burden is light." I do not readily understand or receive what you may have taught during a particular lesson, but I thank God for His Word and the way in which you present it to the Body. Thank you for K.I.S.S. That is my favorite principle of operation. K.I.S.S. — Keep it simple, stupid.

When we returned to Dallas, our little spirits were really sagging. We knew in our hearts we wanted to be here, but we couldn't afford to be out of His will. So back to Dallas we went.

As we drove home from the airport that evening, we sat silently almost all the way. Then my husband said, "We're going to Los Angeles." A big grin came on my face and I said, "Yes, I know."

Then he said, "I don't know how we're going to get there, but we're going." ...We expressed to the Father our desire to come to Crenshaw and asked whether it was His will for our lives. A few days later, in the course of my daily Bible study, I came to the 8th chapter of Deuteronomy. It was like, Wow! Rhema!

I jumped up and ran to show my husband. Immediately, we received it in our hearts as confirmation. We thanked God for it and immediately began confessing "We're going to Crenshaw!"

Well, time passed, and it looked like nothing was happening at all, but everyday we kept saying, "Lord, we thank You that we're in fellowship with Pastor Price and Crenshaw." I think we started applying every principle and confession of faith that the Father had taught us through you.

Then one day, opportunity knocked! My husband received a new job offer. But there was one major hitch. We would have to relocate to where, of all places, Los Angeles! We nearly went through the roof! I think we danced in the Spirit for days!

We made our pre-move trip that spring and got everything ready to go, including putting our house on the market. I need not tell you that our adversary, the devil, was on the job, too, and he threw out some major glitches, including a company restructuring that put virtually all activity on hold. But we kept thanking God that we are in fellowship with Pastor Price and Crenshaw. We knew that we were not alone. As the FaithDome rose in spite of Satan's attacks, our faith rose, too.

Then, in November, 1987, my husband came home and said, "We're going to L.A." I said, "Yes, I know." He said, "No! You're not listening to me. We're going to Los Angeles!" Then it clicked.

We're going to Los Angeles! We're going to Crenshaw. Fred, it had been almost four years, four whole years of believing and confessing. Even as the actual time for the move got closer, Satan kept verbally threatening us with things like, "Well, you know the company is starting to lay off people. It's awfully stupid to be going out there now with so many things up in the air. And on top of that, everything is so much more expensive. And wow, what about the crime! And besides that, you don't know what to do in an earthquake! Everybody is going to drop off into the ocean, you know."

It got ridiculous, but our reply was "No! None of that matters, because we have the victory. When they open the doors to the FaithDome for the first time, we're marching in with the family, yes!"

On Wednesday, September 28, 1988, the confession manifested as we became fellow-shipping members of Crenshaw Christian Center! That was one of the most special times we will ever experience in our lives, because God granted the desires of our heart. As a matter of fact, I felt like it was graduation day all over again.

Unfortunately, it's easy for many saints to believe God for supplying our needs, but many times hold back their faith when it comes to our desires and miss the abundance that God has in store for us.

I am so happy that our family learned to believe and receive the truth that God is willing, not only to meet our needs, but to give us the desires of our hearts, too.

I am so glad that we chose to take heed to the Word of faith, because faith works. My husband has learned to take no thought in the affairs of our lives, and is now blessed more than we had believed in his new job. Our son attends Frederick K.C. Price School, which the Father raised up and anointed with the vision for excellence....

This ministry is so much more than lights and cameras.... We are personally grateful for the TV ministry, for through it all, the seed of this desire was sown, watered, and nurtured to fullness. I can't overemphasize how very valuable Crenshaw Christian Center and Ever Increasing Faith are in the Body of Christ.... We thank the Lord Jesus Christ that He chose to call you, Pastor and Mrs. Price, not only servant, but friend. We love you. To God be all the glory, honor, majesty and power for ever and ever. Amen.

The Word Works! Faith Works! Confession Works! Death and Life are in the Power of the Tongue!!

I say it again, unless you are willing and faithful to press through with your confession and believe they are yours, you will not personally receive all of the provisions and blessings that are available in the Word of God.

If a thief tried to take your belongings, would you resist? Of course you would. But it is amazing how Christians will let the devil take what belongs to them without any resistance. They roll over and play dead, like a dog and let Satan take everything that belongs to them.

SATAN IS A THIEF AND A ROBBER, AND YOU HAVE TO RESIST HIM! You have to stand against him or he will steal what belongs to you. Again, it is by faith that you stand against him. Christians will say, "Praise the Lord, if this is for me, I will get it. And if it is not for me, I won't." That kind of thinking and talking does not work. That is not biblically sound thinking.

Remember, the Bible says, "It is not God's will that any should perish, but that all should come to repentance." Why is it not God's will that any should perish? Because John 3:16 says, **For God so loved the world, that he gave his only begotten Son, that whosoever believeth in him should not perish, but have everlasting life.**

Even though it is not God's will that any perish, folk are perishing. Why? Because it is not up to God whether they perish or not. It is up to God to provide them a method by which they will not perish, but whether they perish or not is based upon their decision, their volitional faith act of taking advantage of what God has supplied.

Satan will steal from you every minute of every day unless you stand up and fight for your rights, and there is nothing God can do. The reason I say there is nothing God can do is because He has already done it. Now the responsibility is in your hands. He has given you all the tools necessary to do something about it. If I do not do something about it, that is my fault.

When my car was delivered from England, I was notified to come down to the dealer and pick up the car. When I did so, I was given the papers and the keys. I could have sat right there in the parking lot for the next ten years. That would have been on me. They had done their part, and it was up to me to drive the car home. God, through His Word, has delivered to you your "car." You have the owner's papers, the keys, license tags, everything. Now, it is up to you to drive it. If you do not drive it, you will sit there in the garage of your life and do nothing.

John 10:10:

> **The thief cometh not, but for to steal, and to kill, and to destroy: I am come that they might have life, and that they might have it more abundantly.**

The will of Jesus for me is abundant life. But if I want it, I will have to confess it. And you will never get it unless you confess it, because Satan will steal it from you. He will steal anything from you that he can.

Understand how he works: He does not walk into a room with a red suit on and a pitchfork in his hand and say, "I'm the devil and I'm here to steal your blessings." No, it will come through the system, through the circumstances.

Until you *confess* in faith that all of what God clearly declares is yours, you will never get it. Satan will keep you spiritually and materially bound and poor and without the things that constitute abundant life.

I do not know *how* confession works, and I do not really care. I am just glad that it works.

Worrying Is Sin

1 Peter 5:7:

Casting all your care upon him; for he careth for you.

If you are a caring person, you have things that concern you — children, parents, wives, husbands, families, jobs, professions, and homes. These things do not always work correctly, so they cause concern, and sometimes that concern gets right down to worry.

Many people, including Christians, operate in constant, on-going worry. They are so concerned until it affects their ability to function on a daily basis. First Peter 5:7 is a scripture we should confess. If we do not, Satan will steal our peace of mind.

Casting means to "throw away from you." Casting ALL — so how much is left? NONE! It is interesting that most Christians would never think of drinking a can of beer or a cocktail, because they consider *that* to be sinful. They would never steal anything, because they would consider that to be a sin. But they worry constantly and think nothing about it being a sin.

The reason for that is because everybody worries, generally speaking, and since they do, it is an accepted method of dealing with the issues of life. But, IT IS A SIN TO WORRY! Why? Because when I worry, I am calling God a liar. I am saying, "Heavenly Father, Your Word is no good. You do not care about Your children, and You do not take care of Your family."

If you believed Him, why would you be worrying? Worry is your attempt to do something about the situation, which means you are not satisfied to let God do it. That is what worry is. It is a lack of trust. It is a lack of faith. You do not need any faith to worry. Do you understand that?

I used to be a world champion worrier. In fact, I worried so much until I worried a hole in my stomach, called a peptic ulcer. I could not eat and keep any food on my stomach. I worried *all* the time. I worried about everything and was uptight all the time. I was trying to solve all my problems, and they were too big for me.

When I found out how to walk by faith, I retired from worrying! When I found out how to walk in accord with God's Word, some 20 years ago, I stopped worrying.

Do not misunderstand me, there are things for which I am responsible, things I am accountable for, but I do not worry about them. I do my part, then leave it in the hands of the Lord. For instance, the FaithDome. It took from July, 1977 to July, 1986 — nine years — to get in position to build the FaithDome. And then it took an additional three years to actually construct it! If it had been me building that Dome, it would have been built in a year. I would have worked 24 hours a day on it. But I could not do it and I knew it. I did not lose any sleep over it. I resigned myself to the fact that if it never got finished, it was not my problem, it was God's.

I did my part. The rest was up to the Lord to work through people to get the job done. I cast all my care on Him because He cares for me. I confessed that the FaithDome was built, and I did not worry one second through it all.

If you are still worried, you have not cast it on Him. And He will not get involved until you cast it. Now Satan will back you into a corner if you let him, saying "What are you going to do if so-and-so does not happen?" "What will people say if they come and repossess your car?" You have to resist him and fight him with his own tactics. For instance, tell him, "I'll tell you what they will say, Devil, they repossessed my car. So what? That is not the last car they will make. I will get another one."

If you know how to believe God, your car will not be repossessed. But, what I am saying is that you must learn to fight the devil on his own terms, or else he will intimidate you with worry. Confession must become a way of life if you want to enjoy and experience what we have in Christ. In order for this to work on the highest level, you have to be CONSISTENT, FAITHFUL, UNMOVABLE, UNSHAKABLE, UNBENDABLE.

Matthew 8:17 tells us something else that we possess in Christ:

> **That it might be fulfilled which was spoken by Esaias the prophet, saying, Himself took our infirmities, and bare our sicknesses.**

This is referring to Jesus. It says He took our infirmities, and bore our sicknesses. It is obvious that if He bore my sicknesses, He does not want me to bear them. So I retired from sicknesses and disease 20 years ago. It does not belong to me.

That does not mean you are not going to be attacked, because that is what Ephesians 6 is all about when it says "Put on the whole armor of God, that you may be able to stand against the evil one." Take the shield of faith wherewith you shall be able to quench all the fiery darts of the wicked one. Why? Because the darts are going to come. Sickness and disease are some of the darts. If you are a Christian, then you have a right to be well. It is not God's will for you to be sick. Many Christians have strange ideas. They figure that if you do not get sick or get killed in some kind of calamity, how are you going to die? Well, have you ever thought about wearing out? You do not have to get sick to die. Divine healing and divine health are your possession, but you have to confess it.

When I feel bad, I do not confess I feel bad, but I confess I believe I am healed. I do not deny that I am feeling bad, but rather, I do not talk about it.

2 Corinthians 4:18:

While we look not at the things which are seen, but at the things which are not seen: for the things which are seen are temporal (or temporary and subject to change); **but the things which are not seen are eternal.**

He did not say that the things that are seen do not exist. He said, DO NOT LOOK AT THEM. If you do not look at them, what do you do? Ignore them. And how do you do that? The same way you ignore anyone when you do not want to be bothered. Ignore the sickness the same way. Act like it is not there.

YOU DO NOT SAY IT IS NOT THERE. When you ignore somebody, you are not saying that they are not there. You are just not giving them any credit for having anything to do with you at that moment in time. When you ignore someone, you do not deny they are there, you simply do not talk to them. That is what you have to do with sickness and disease.

What I have said is not some kind of psychological, mental approach. It is a spiritual law. Just because we have never heard something before does not invalidate it or make it cultish, or something out of line with the Word of God.

I have been married for nearly 39 years, and I did not find out about the law of confession until after the first 17 years of my marriage. I operated in that law of confession all of those years. However, the first 17 years were lived in a negative environment created by my own confession. Instead of governing what I said with my mouth, I said whatever I felt, whatever I saw, and whatever I could figure out with my mind. I did not confess what the Word said.

Now that I look back on it, it is interesting to see that I actually experienced in my everyday life the sum total of what I had been confessing. You have to understand that laws work whether you know they are working or not. Although you may not know that there is such a thing as the law of confession, it does not make any difference, it works anyway. If you are on the negative side of that law, it will work for you in a negative way and produce negative results in your life. And then you will end up thinking that it is the will of God, when it is not.

However, you control your circumstance by your confession, and that, of course, is based on your faith in terms of what you believe.

At the beginning of this book, I told you that we are whatever the Word of God says we are, whether we are experiencing that or not. If God says we have it, we have it. And whatever God says we can do, we can do.

If you do not get in line with God's estimate of you, you will go down below the level of who you really are and there is nothing God can do about it, because He has already done it through Christ. I have to know it, believe it, and confess it, then it will begin to happen in my life.

Matthew 8:17:

That it might be fulfilled which was spoken by Esaias the prophet, saying, Himself took our infirmities, and bare our sicknesses.

You need to make that personal. It says "our," but our means the Body of Christ. I am a member of the Body of Christ, so I could reduce this down to a personal level. Jesus took our (my) infirmities, so that says He does not want me to have them.

Romans 5:17:

For if by one man's offence death reigned by one; much more they which receive abundance of grace and of the gift of righteousness shall REIGN IN LIFE BY ONE, JESUS CHRIST.

He said I should reign in life as a king, not as a welfare recipient. IN LIFE, not in heaven, not in the sweet by and by, over there on the other side, after while, but over here on *this* side.

Do you know what that will do to you when you begin to confess that about yourself? It will change your mentality. It will change your estimate of who you are. Instead of going into a store and going downstairs to the bargain basement, you will get on the elevator and go up to the top floor, because that is where kings shop!

He said I SHOULD REIGN AS A KING IN LIFE! CHRISTIANITY HAS BEEN SOLD A BILL OF GOODS. The Church of the Lord Jesus Christ, by and large, operates on the basis of the poverty syndrome. The devil told us that we are supposed to be poor in this life, because we are going to get our wealth over on the other side. But that is not true.

The Bible says that it is impossible for God to lie, so the only alternative is that God must tell the truth. Therefore, if God tells me that I am a king, I must be a king. When I first found this out, I did not look like one and I sure had nothing that would place me in a kingly category. But I began to see myself sitting on a throne. Sitting on the throne of my own life, not reigning and ruling over somebody else and dictating to them, but reigning over my own life.

I began to see myself that way, even when I did not have a dime, and could not pay my bills. I was struggling. My struggles had struggles! But I began to see myself as a king. I began to see the blessings of God pouring out to me. Since I am a king, I should be treated as a king. I should receive tribute like a king receives tribute.

Example: I was sitting in my office one day minding my own business. A minister called and made an appointment to see me through my secretary. He had some questions about ministry that he wanted to ask me about.

He asked me his questions and then before leaving, he said, "I want to give you something." I said, "All right, praise the Lord, I receive." He reached into his pocket and pulled out a check and handed it to me. He said, "Brother Price, the Lord told me last year to give you a certain amount of money." I never asked him for that money, but since I am a king, I am supposed to receive tribute. Of course, I have all the other things in place. I am giving, I am tithing, I am living right, doing everything I know to do based on God's Word.

He said, "This is the first installment on what the Lord told me to give you." The check was for $5,000. He said, "The Lord told me to give you $10,000." I said to him, "I believe every word of it." It *had* to be the Lord. It could not have been the devil!

When was the last time somebody gave you $5,000? Here is my point: Before I started confessing God's Word over my life, no one ever gave me $5, let alone $5,000! They did not give me anything except bills — a notice that they were about to repossess my car. And another notice telling me they were about to repossess my television set. I got those kinds of things. Nobody ever gave me $5,000. Now, that happens fairly regularly — not every day or every week, but it happens.

But it never happened until I started seeing myself as a king. Revelation 1:6 tells us that Jesus ...**hath made us kings and priests unto God and his Father....** I am supposed to receive tribute. I just took God at His Word.

I am a giver. I live to give. And I look forward to the day when I can give away a million dollars at a shot, for the ministry, to help the Kingdom of God. As soon as I was given that $5,000, instantaneously my mind began to compute my tithe. I do that whenever I get anything. I do not think of how I can spend the money, but rather how much will the tithe be?

He said I should reign as a king in life. When I awake each morning, I look in the mirror and say, "Good morning, King Frederick, what is on the agenda for today? What new victories are we going to experience?"

11

#4 — What We Can Do In Christ

The fourth truth we must learn if we are to live victoriously in this life is "What We Can Do In Christ." This has to do with our empowering and our ability. You have ability through Jesus Christ in God, ability way beyond your wildest dreams, beyond what tradition, theology, and religious rituals have told you.

We have not been taught about our ability, yet the Bible is full of it. You can do everything that the Word of God says you can do. When you say what God's Word says, you are saying what God says. You are simply mimicking, or copying God.

More has been proclaimed from the pulpit about what we cannot do than about what we can do. We cannot do this, we cannot eat this, we cannot go there, we cannot wear this, we cannot comb our hair this way, we cannot, we cannot, we cannot! That is most of what we Christians have heard. But that is not what the Word of God says.

EVERYTHING THAT THE WORD OF GOD SAYS YOU CAN DO, YOU CAN DO. But you will *never* be able to do more than you are willing to confess that you can do, based upon God's revealed Word. It is confession through faith that ignites and activates God's power in your life. We are not talking about saying positive things for the sake of being positive. Being positive is better than being negative, but that is not what God is talking about. We are talking about the trigger that releases the bullet, the power of God — and it just so happens to be words — *confession*.

Let me repeat it: You will *never* be able to do more than you are willing to confess that you can do, based on the Word of God. Why? Because of this simple principle:

Proverbs 6:2:

Thou art snared with the words of thy mouth, thou art taken with the words of thy mouth.

That is a powerful scripture. A snare is a trap. So, in modern language, we could say it this way. *Thou art trapped with the words of thy mouth.*

If your words are words that limit you, then you will be limited. If your words are words that are contrary to what the Bible says about you, then you will be trapped.

Now you can see the clever, insidious plot that Satan has contrived over the years and has infiltrated into the churches, to keep the Word of God, the Bible, out of the churches, thus out of the hands of God's people. We must confess God's Word.

Philippians 4:13:

I can do all things through Christ which (or, who) **strengtheneth me.**

The *all things* are based upon what God says in His Word. I can do all things *that God says I can do.* I cannot just do all things, because I cannot have a baby. I could say, "I am going to get pregnant," but that would be a dumb confession, which would not work.

Again, I can do all things through Christ who strengthens me, based on what God's Word declares, not just on some fantasy that you come up with out of the clear blue. This is the kind of mentality you have to develop, and you can develop that through the power of positive confession. It will change your life. Your circumstances will change. It is amazing how words will change the environment.

At first you may say, "This guy must be crazy. What is he talking about, words changing the environment?" Well, think about this, when a nation's leaders, whether a king, prime minister, or president, declare we are at war, those words change your environment. Your whole scope of living changes just by words.

Realize that when a man and woman stand before me as a minister, and I say, "Will you take this woman to be your wedded wife?" he could say, "No!" and he would stay in his same environment. But when he says, "Yes," "I will," or, "I do," his life will change. WORDS changed it.

That is a common thing that we just take for granted, but if you start looking around, examining your whole life, everything eventually revolves back to something you got into by your words.

The virginity of some women was changed by their words. They did not know he was lying when he said, "I love you." He said he had never loved anyone as much as he loved you. Then he said, "Baby, if you *really love me* . . ." and your virginity went out the window. He put his pants on, buttoned up his coat, slipped his belt around his waist, and said, "Bye-bye." *WORDS!*

You never would have gotten into that mess if it had not been for words. I love you, I love you, I love you. That is what started it. You think about it. Many things go back to words.

Even right now, for many of you, your lives are a caldron of apparent hopelessness because way back in time somebody that you had a lot of confidence in, like a mother or a father, said, "You ain't no good, and you will never be any good. You are just like your old daddy. He was no good and you ain't gonna be nothin' either."

Sometimes, comments like that change people for the better, but most of the time, it changes them for the worst.

It crushes their spirits. WORDS!! Just to hear a mother or a father say, "I love you, son, I understand." Or, "You ain't no good. You're a shiftless, good-for-nothing. You are just like your daddy. He was a wino and you are going to end up just like him." Those are horrible words, and lives have been crushed and changed by them.

The Word says "we can do all things...." Do you know that it is actually a sin to limit, by your confession of doubt, what God says you are able to do? Did you know that doubt is a sin? Unbelief is a sin. To disbelieve your Heavenly Father is a sin. You are saying, "Your Word is not true." You are saying, "You do not deal in the truth, Father." It is a sin to limit, by your negative confession, what God says is actually yours in the Word.

Let us examine some examples of your ability and your power in Christ.

Mark 16:17,18:

> And these signs shall follow them that believe; In my name shall they cast out devils; they shall speak with new tongues;

> They shall take up serpents; and if they drink any deadly thing, it shall not hurt them; they shall lay hands on the sick, and they shall recover.

All of these things are positive. That is our ability in Christ, but we have to confess it and then follow that confession by action, by actually doing it. That is why we do that at Crenshaw Christian Center, the church that I pastor. We lay hands on the sick. We cast out demons when it is necessary.

You Must Believe What God Says Is True

Some people say they do not believe in demons. That is fine. No problem. If you are smarter than God, I hope I can get to know you better! First of all, I would like to see the universes that you have created, the one that you are sustaining by your power and might. When you say you do not believe in demons, you are saying that you are smarter than God, because God believes in demons. If God did not believe in demons, He would never give us authority to cast them out.

Demons *must* exist. They are the ones causing all this confusion going on in the world. They are the behind-the-scenes instigators of this confusion. Sometimes they have to be discerned and cast out.

Speak with new tongues, cast out demons, take up serpents (accidentally), drink any deadly thing (unknown) and it shall not hurt us. THAT is our authority and ability, but it will not work unless we confess and then do it.

John 14:12:

> **Verily, verily, I say unto you, He that believeth on me, the works that I do shall he do also; and greater works than these shall he do; because I go unto my Father.**

We should see the same works in the Family of God that we see in the ministry of the Lord Jesus Christ. And yet, how many ministers tell you just the opposite of that, and have no scripture to back it up? The church has swallowed that lie hook, line, sinker — the fishing pole, the reel, the fisherman, and his boots! They say, ''That went out with the early church. Miracles are not for today. That went out when the last apostle died.''

Nowhere in the Bible will you find where it says it went out when the last apostle died. All that is the rationale of man. Do you know why? Because they have not seen the works done. The assumption is that because we have not seen it done, then it is not for us today. It never occurred to them that maybe we are not doing our part in order to qualify for these things to be done.

Notice, Jesus said, THESE SIGNS SHALL FOLLOW THEM THAT BELIEVE. If you do not believe, the signs will not follow. It is not that you should just believe in Jesus, because there are many who believe in Jesus, but they do not believe in the signs. So, to believe in Jesus is where we start, but you have to believe in what He said.

These signs shall follow them that believe; In my name, they shall cast out demons. You have to believe in that. You have to believe in demons and believe in casting them out when they get ugly and act up. Get rid of them. *They shall speak with new tongues* — but you will not if you do not believe it. *They shall lay hands on the sick and they shall recover;* but they will not if you do not believe it. Because if you do not believe it, you will not lay hands on them. And the qualification is that they cannot recover until hands are laid on them by them who believe.

The works that I do shall he do also and greater works than these shall he do because I go to my Father. We cannot do greater works in terms of *quality,* but we will do greater works in terms of *quantity,* because there are more of us than there were of Jesus. Understand that Jesus, at the time He walked the earth, was the only *body* (body of Christ) on earth that was filled with the Holy Ghost. The Bible says that He had the Spirit without measure; therefore, as an individual person, He would be able to do greater things than we would ever do as individuals.

The Holy Ghost is not in me alone, but in every born-again, Spirit-filled believer. Each of us is only one infinitesimal part of the Body of Christ, so I can only do an infinitesimal part of what Jesus could do, because when He walked the earth, He was the only Body of Christ that was filled with the Holy Ghost.

He had all of the power working in Him, so He could do more things as an individual person than you or I could ever do as an individual person. God has not limited His Spirit just to Fred Price. But His Spirit is in the Body of Christ, not just in the body of Price. So, collectively, we can do greater works because there are *more* of us. Greater in quantity, not greater in quality. After you have raised the dead, that is a hard act to follow!!

Think about this. Jesus had two hands and, at the very most, He could only lay hands on two people at the same time and get them healed. But we are in the Body of Christ, and we have tens of thousands of hands. It is conceivable that we could lay hands on ten thousand people at one moment in time, when He could only lay hands on two. Therefore, we would be doing greater works quantitatively, but not qualitatively.

This is what we have; this is who we are, this is what we can do, and we have to confess it and do it, if we want to experience it.

Matthew 17:20:

> **And Jesus said unto them, Because of your unbelief: for verily I say unto you, If ye have faith as a grain of mustard seed, ye shall say unto this mountain, Remove hence to yonder place; and it shall remove; and nothing shall be impossible unto you.**

Nothing shall be impossible unto you sounds like I can do all things through Christ. It is the same thing. Now understand this, nothing shall be impossible unto you *that God has said you can do*, because if "nothing" is impossible, I return to my original analysis, which is that I ought to be able to get pregnant and have a baby. But I cannot, because I am not designed that way. Everything God says I can do, I can — but I have to believe that and confess it. I have to make it a part of my everyday life.

We Are Overcomers

1 John 5:4:

> **For whatsoever is born of God overcometh the world: and this is the victory that overcometh the world, even our faith.**

In the sight of our Father, we are overcomers. Right away, you can see that something is radically wrong among the ranks of Christianity. If we can overcome, then there should never be Christians getting divorces, because you have everything with which to win. "Well, she was not right for me," or, "he was not right for me." Wait a minute! You *said* they were not and that is why they were not. You can love anyone you want to love. Love is something you *do*. It is not automatic.

You have to purpose to love someone. You might have some feelings or emotions, but that is not love. You can look at someone and they can look good to you and you can get feelings about it. But that does not mean you are in love. You might be in *lust*, but not necessarily in love. You choose to love. It is a choice you make, but once made, you will have to work at it.

Marriage does not happen by itself. The Christians that know the Word and learn who they are in Christ and what they can do in Christ and confess that, can make a marriage work. And when I say "make it work," I do not mean to tolerate and exist in a relationship that you hate every minute. What I am telling you is that you can get together and work it out and that will be the best woman for you and that will be the best man for you.

Do not tell me you cannot do it, because if you say you cannot do it, then that verse lied when it said, ...**this is the victory that overcometh the world, even our faith** (1 John 5:4). By your faith, you can overcome a bad marriage. You can overcome anything that Satan has brought against you in your total life. But you will have to believe it, and begin to confess it and then act in concert with it.

My Father is the One Who told me I am an overcomer. If I say I am not, then I am in contradiction to my Father. God cannot lie! If He says I can overcome the world, then I can overcome it. I may not be overcoming it, but that is not God's fault. That is MY fault. Again, this is not a psyche job, this is the power of *positive confession*. This is what the Word says is yours. You have to see yourself as a victor. You have to see yourself with victory. You have to see yourself overcoming, and then do not let any circumstance or any person — your wife or your husband — tell you anything else.

You are an overcomer. But you will have to fight. The Bible tells you, **Fight the good fight of faith.** You have to fight, and fighting is bloody, and fighting hurts, but we WIN! WE WIN!

Say this out loud: "I AM A WORLD OVERCOMER." Romans 10:17 says ...**faith cometh by hearing....** That is why you have to say it. That is what people do not understand, and they will accuse you of bragging. But when I say that, I am not bragging. What I am doing is putting the law of God into operation. You see, if I want faith for the fact that I am a world overcomer to come to me, I have to say it. Because another law is, ...**faith cometh by hearing, and hearing by the Word of God.**

When I say that I am a world overcomer, I am speaking the Word of God, because the Word of God says, ...**and this is the victory that overcometh the world, even our faith...** (1 John 5:4), so I have to *say* that. When I first began saying that, I could not beat a fly! Circumstances had me defeated. But I began saying it, "I am a world overcomer!" I would go to bed at night and dream about overcoming the world. I would get up in the morning and say it again. I kept saying it until it became a part of me.

At first it was very imperceptible, but then all of a sudden, I woke up one morning and realized I had won some victories. Oooh! It tasted so good! And then you get a holy boldness, and you will not accept defeat from anyone. That is THE POWER OF POSITIVE CONFESSION!!

First John 5:4 again:

For whatsoever is born of God overcometh the world: and THIS IS THE VICTORY THAT OVERCOMETH THE WORLD, EVEN OUR FAITH.

Who is he that overcometh the world? FRED PRICE. Put your name in there. He is talking about YOU. Who is *he?* Who is *she?* Who are *they* that overcometh the world?

We found out from Proverbs 6:2 that *we are snared by the words of our mouths.* So we need to be very careful about what we let come out of our mouths.

Jesus said in Matthew 12:37, **For by thy WORDS thou shalt be justified, and by thy WORDS thou shalt be condemned.** BY YOUR WORDS! Do you see that?

Matthew 12:37:

For by thy words thou shalt be justified, and by thy words thou shalt be condemned.

Proverbs 18:21:

Death and life are in the power of the tongue. . . .

Proverbs 6:2:

Thou art snared with the words of thy mouth, thou art taken with the words of mouth.

We can win through Jesus Christ. But you cannot do it passively. YOU CANNOT BE A PACIFIST AND WIN IN THIS BATTLE! You must believe, you must act on what you believe, you must confess what you believe. Start NOW. THE POWER OF POSITIVE CONFESSION *works!!*

Dr. Frederick K.C. Price founded Crenshaw Christian Center in Los Angeles, California, in 1973 with a congregation of some 300 people. Today, the church's membership numbers well over 12,500 people of various racial backgrounds.

Crenshaw Crhistian Center, home of the renowned 10,140-seat FaithDome, has a staff of some 200 employees, and consists of a School of Ministry; School of the Bible; a Helps Ministry Summer School; the Frederick K.C. Price, III Elementary and Junior High School; and a Child Care Center.

"EVER INCREASING FAITH" Television and Radio broadcasts are outreaches of Crenshaw Christian Center. The television program is viewed on more than 100 stations throughout the United States and overseas. The radio program is aired on approximately 60 stations across the country.

Dr. Price travels extensively teaching the WORD OF FAITH simply and understandably in the power of the Holy Spirit. He is the author of several books on faith and divine healing. In 1990, he founded the "FELLOWSHIP OF INNER-CITY WORD OF FAITH MINISTRIES (FICWFM)" for the purpose of fostering and spreading the faith message among independent ministries located in the urban, metropolitan areas of the United States.

For a complete list of tapes and books by Fred Price,
or to receive his publication, *Ever Increasing Faith
Messenger*, write:

Fred Price
Crenshaw Christian Center
P. O. Box 90000
Los Angeles, CA 90009